DRAW COMICS
AND GRAPHIC NOVELS

ARCTURUS

ARCTURUS

This edition published in 2017 by Arcturus Publishing Limited
26/27 Bickels Yard, 151–153 Bermondsey Street,
London SE1 3HA

ISBN: 978-1-78428-307-0
CH005163US
Supplier 26, Date 0217, Print run 5413

Editors: William Potter, Joe Harris, and Kate Overy
Authors: Frank Lee, William Potter, Lisa Regan, and Joe Harris
Illustrations: Anthony Williams, Leo Campos, Seb Camagajevac, Nigel
Dobbyn, David Belmonte, Peter Gray, Frank Lee, and Jim Hansen
Cover Illustration: Juan Calle
Design: Duck Egg Blue
Cover Design: Peter Ridley

Printed in China

CONTENTS

PART 1: THE WORLD OF COMICS

SUPERHERO COMICS

Superheroes first exploded on to the American comics scene in the 1930s and 40s. Superman, the first of these larger-than-life characters, arrived in Action Comics #1 in 1938. Superheroes made such a huge impact on the medium that today, many people equate comics with superhero stories.

SCIENCE FICTION COMICS

Science fiction comics were very popular in the 1930s, and it was from this genre that superheroes emerged. Sci-fi comics have continued to be especially popular in the UK, where comic fans thrill at the weekly adventures of futuristic antiheroes such as Judge Dredd.

FANTASY COMICS

Comics are the perfect medium for fantasy adventures, since artists don't need to worry about special-effects budgets. The number of exotic locations and weird creatures featured in a story are limited only by the storyteller's imagination! Get ready to unleash a whole army of orcs, trolls, and dragons on your unsuspecting readers.

MANGA COMICS

"Manga" isn't really a genre so much as a nationality, since all comics from Japan fall into this category. Modern manga first emerged in the wake of World War II, during the American occupation of Japan. The style was initially influenced by American cartoonists such as Walt Disney, but it has since developed an entirely unique approach.

HORROR COMICS

Horror comics with fantastic names like Vault of Horror or Tales from the Crypt were hugely popular in the 1940s and 50s. Comics can't make people jump with a bang, like a movie can. However, a talented artist can create an eerie and sinister atmosphere that will chill readers to the bone.

TOOLS OF THE TRADE

YOU DON'T NEED LOTS OF EXPENSIVE EQUIPMENT TO START CREATING COMICS. YOU CAN START WITH JUST A PEN AND PAPER! THE MOST IMPORTANT TOOL IS YOUR OWN IMAGINATION.

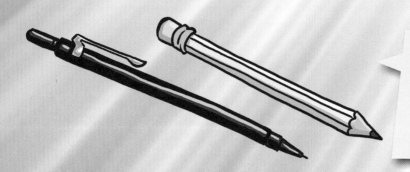

PENCILS
Soft (B, 2B) pencils are great for drawing loosely and are easy to erase. Fine-point pencils are handy for adding detail.

ERASERS
A kneaded eraser molds to shape, so you can use it to remove pencil from tiny areas. Keep a clean, square-edged eraser to hand, too.

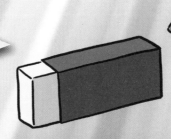

PENS
An artist's pens are his or her most precious tools! Gather a selection with different tips for varying the thickness of your line work.

PAPER
Good quality paper will make your artwork look professional, but you can draw your rough sketches on any scrap of paper to hand.

FINE LINE AND BRUSH PENS

Fine line pens are excellent for small areas of detail. Brush pens are perfect for varying your line weight or shading large areas.

CIRCLE TEMPLATES

Very few people can draw a perfect circle freehand, so a set of circle templates is a good buy. If you don't have any templates, you can draw round various everyday items such as coins, cups, and jar lids to create your circles.

CURVE TEMPLATES

A set of artist's curves is an inexpensive aid to drawing curved shapes of various sizes and angles. Many sets of curves include circular templates cut out of the centers of the curves so they can be used for drawing circles, too.

PENCILING SKILLS

THE KEY TO CREATING GREAT GRAPHIC-NOVEL ART IS TO START WITH SIMPLE SHAPES AND VERY GRADUALLY BUILD UP DETAIL. LET'S START BY LOOKING AT SHAPES SUCH AS CYLINDERS, CUBES, AND SPHERES. IF YOU LEARN HOW TO GIVE THREE-DIMENSIONAL FORM TO SIMPLE SHAPES (LIKE THE ONES BELOW), YOU WILL HAVE UNLOCKED THE REAL SECRET TO DRAWING LIFELIKE FIGURES.

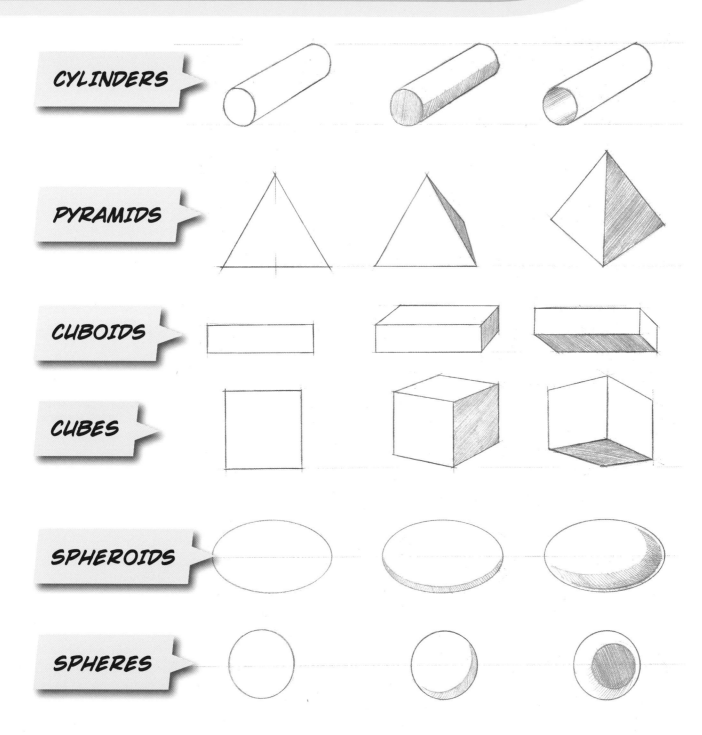

CYLINDERS

PYRAMIDS

CUBOIDS

CUBES

SPHEROIDS

SPHERES

BUILDING A BODY

To create a human figure, you should start with a stick figure, then build on it using simple shapes. To achieve other poses, you just need to reposition these simple shapes. Once you have mastered this step-by-step technique, you'll have the skills you need to draw realistic figures with ease.

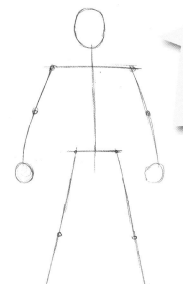

STEP 1

Start by drawing a simple stick figure as your frame. The figure should have shoulders and hips.

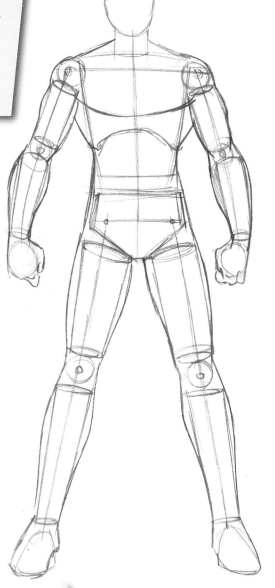

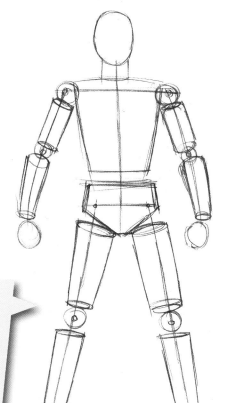

STEP 2

Now build your body by adding basic shapes to the stick figure.

STEP 3

Draw around the shapes to produce your figure outline. Once you have established your character's body shape, you can add details.

DRAWING BODIES

YOUR COMIC CHARACTERS MAY COME FROM YOUR IMAGINATION, BUT THEIR BODY SHAPES WILL BE BASED ON REALITY. HERE ARE SOME RULES FOR PROPORTIONS THAT YOU CAN USE AS A GUIDE WHEN DRAWING.

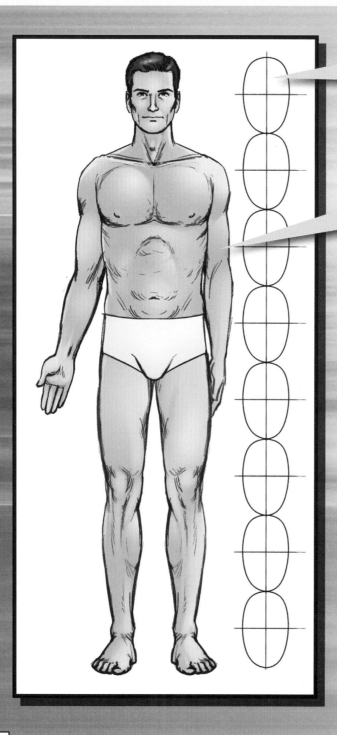

HEADS
Measure characters in "head heights". Typically, a person is eight times the height of their head, from top to toe.

ARMS
Make sure your character's arms are in proportion. Straightened, they should reach down to mid-thigh level.

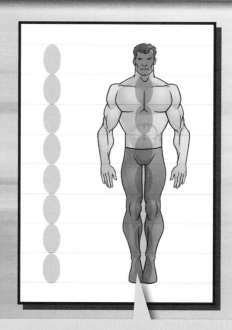

SUPERHEROIC BODIES
Superheroes have extra-broad shoulders, thick necks, and powerful arm muscles.

WOMEN HAVE A MORE SLENDER BUILD THAN MEN, WITH MUSCLES THAT ARE LESS DEFINED. THE NECK IS LONGER AND THE WAIST MORE PRONOUNCED. FEMALE CHARACTERS FOLLOW THE SAME "EIGHT HEADS" PRINCIPLE.

TORSOS

The distance from shoulder to hips should be about two-and-a-half "head heights".

SHOULDERS AND HIPS

Female characters' hips and shoulders are similar in width. Males taper from broad shoulders to a more narrow waist and hips.

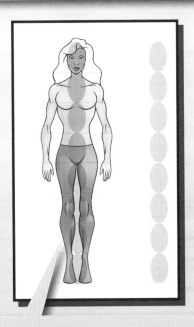

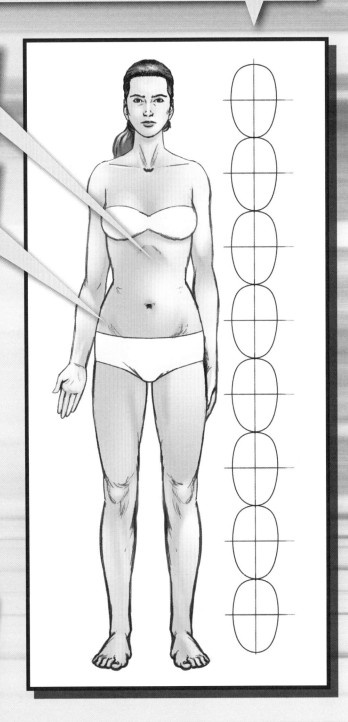

SUPERHEROINES

Superheroines do not have such large muscles as male superheroes, but their shoulders are broader than real women's.

DRAWING HEADS

THE HUMAN HEAD CAN BE MAPPED OUT USING A RECTANGULAR GRID (SEE BELOW). THIS EXAMPLE IS BASED ON A STANDARD-SIZED HEAD, BUT YOU CAN ALTER THESE PROPORTIONS WHEN CREATING CHARACTERS WITH DIFFERENT LOOKS, SUCH AS MONSTERS OR SUPERNATURAL BEINGS.

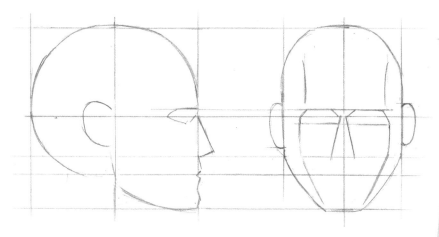

GETTING STARTED

First divide the rectangle into smaller shapes, as shown here. Note that the forehead makes up half the height of the head. Position the eyes on the center line. The nose should extend downward from the center line. The ears should be on the same level as the nose.

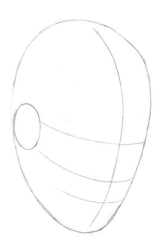

TRY DRAWING OTHER ANGLES

Once you have learned these basic steps, try drawing the head from other angles and adding new details.

FLESHING OUT YOUR PENCILS

Once you are happy with the basic pose and attitude of your character, you can start to add more detail.

CLEANING UP

Draw an outline around your basic shapes. Then, remove the shapes to leave a clean outline. Now you can add detail. Develop your character's hair, clothing, and muscle tone. Think about his facial expression. It may help to use a mirror, or have a friend pose for you.

SHADOWS

Pencil in areas of light and shade to add depth to your drawing. This will look even more effective once it's inked.

FACIAL EXPRESSIONS

THE BEST COMIC-BOOK STORYTELLERS ARE MASTERS OF FACIAL EXPRESSIONS. FACES COMMUNICATE YOUR CHARACTERS' FEELINGS, MOTIVATIONS, AND PERSONALITIES. THE BEST WAY TO PRACTICE EXPRESSIONS IS TO USE A MIRROR OR ASK A VOLUNTEER TO MODEL FOR YOU.

This superhero's smile is friendly, relaxed, and confident. He looks trustworthy and carefree.

This cop's expression is angry but determined. Unlike the superhero, he looks as if he is carrying the weight of the world on his shoulders.

GLOATING

DOWNBEAT

There are as many facial expressions as there are emotions! Here are some common ones for you to practice.

DETERMINED

IN LOVE

ENRAGED

SCORNFUL

BODY POSTURE

THE WAY A PERSON STANDS OR MOVES CAN SAY AS MUCH ABOUT THEM AS THEIR FACE. YOU WILL NEED TO MAKE YOUR CHARACTERS PERFORM LIKE ACTORS! BY SHOWING HOW THEY RESPOND TO A SITUATION, YOU CAN MAKE READERS CARE ABOUT WHAT IS HAPPENING TO THEM.

RELAXED

This character looks cool, calm, and collected. Her arms are hanging loosely, and there is no tension in her shoulders or elbows. She has a warm and open smile.

NERVOUS

This woman's wide eyes and raised hands show she is worried about something. Her shoulders are tense and she leans forward, ready to run if necessary.

SCARED

This guy is terrified! He has thrown up his hands to ward off danger and his eyebrows have shot right up. His eyes and mouth show his fear. He looks like he is ready to leap backward.

CONFIDENT

If this dude is scared, he's not showing it! With his feet apart and his hands curled into fists, he's ready to take on any threat. The determined look on his face says he's a hero.

PERSPECTIVE

NOW YOU NEED TO CREATE A WORLD FOR YOUR CHARACTERS TO INHABIT. TO MAKE YOUR SCENERY REALISTIC AND BELIEVABLE, A BASIC KNOWLEDGE OF PERSPECTIVE IS NECESSARY.

If we continue these lines, they will eventually meet (Fig. 3). The point at which they meet determines the horizon line. This is called a one-point perspective because the lines meet at a single point (Fig. 4).

VANISHING POINT AND HORIZON LINE

Look at the diagram of a train track, below (Fig. 1). Notice how the rails get closer together the further they go into the distance. The point where the lines join is called the vanishing point. The horizontal line in the distance is called the horizon line. The horizon line is the viewer's eye level.

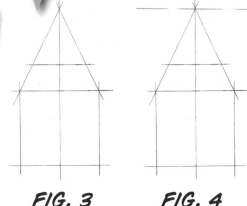

FIG. 3   FIG. 4

FIG. 5

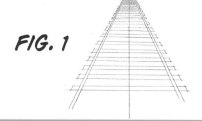

FIG. 1

PLOTTING PERSPECTIVE

Let's take a simple cube (Fig. 2A) and look at how the rules of perspective apply.

When we turn the cube so we are looking directly at one of the corners, we get a two-point perspective (Fig. 5). This means there are two vanishing points.

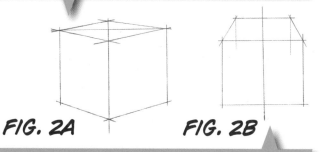

FIG. 2A   FIG. 2B

FIG. 6

Take the cube and turn it so we are looking at it straight on (Fig. 2B). Draw a line down the middle. Notice that the two sides on the top appear to be drawing closer together toward the back.

Here is the cube from above (Fig. 6). If we follow the converging lines to their ultimate meeting point, we again get a two-point perspective.

USING PERSPECTIVE IN YOUR COMIC ART

Here are some examples of how to apply the rules of perspective to comic-book panels. Even though it's tricky, it's important to try to get the perspective right. To make the scenes in your comic book look as realistic as possible, all the elements in the foreground, background, and center of your page must be positioned correctly. When you have multiple vanishing points, attach another sheet of paper to your drawing so that you can continue the perspective lines off the page to get them just right.

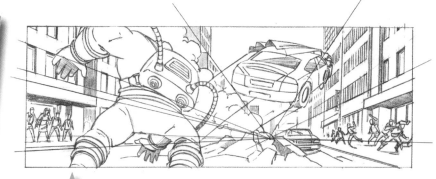

This scene has been drawn using a one-point perspective.

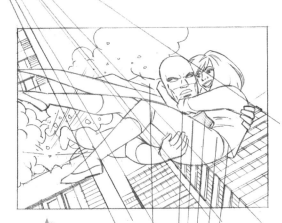

This example has a two-point perspective.

Another example of a two-point perspective.

INKING AND COLORING

THE JADE DRAGON

A CLEAN, CRISP LINE STYLE HAS BEEN USED TO INK THIS CHARACTER, BUT YOU MAY WISH TO EXPERIMENT WITH DIFFERENT STYLES AND TEXTURES OF YOUR OWN. COLOR HAS BEEN APPLIED IN LAYERS FOR A RICH FINISH.

There are a number of ways to ink a pencil drawing. Some artists prefer to use a brush and a pot of black Indian ink. We recommend that you use waterproof Indian ink to ink your pencil drawings, so that when you apply color on top, your ink will not raise or smudge. If you decide to use a brush, a no. 3 sable brush can be used to achieve a variety of line thicknesses.

There are also lots of good inking pens available, with a range of nib thicknesses, including superfine, fine, and brush. The brush nib pens are very good as they produce a wide range of line thicknesses, too.

STEP 1
Finish your pencil drawing, marking out any areas of shading to go over in solid, black ink.

STEP 2

Keeping a steady hand, carefully ink over your pencil artwork. Try to make the lines as crisp and precise as you can. The solid areas of black ink will show through after you have applied color.

STEP 3

Start coloring by applying a dark green base to the clothing.

STEP 4

Now apply a medium skin tone. Don't choose a shade that's too dark, as later we'll layer darker tones on top of this color to add shading.

STEP 5

Use a lighter shade of green in the central panels of fabric to break up the areas of dark green. A color called cadmium yellow has been applied to the trim of the suit and the forearm guards.

STEP 6

Finally, shape and tone are added to the skin by using darker, warmer skin tones. The folds in the suit are accentuated by using darker greens with a black or blue hue. A mid-range cool gray has been used for the straps and soles of the boots.

INKING AND COLORING

THE ANNIHILATOR

THIS CHARACTER IS FINISHED USING A VARIETY OF DIFFERENT LINE THICKNESSES AND LAYERS OF COLOR. THESE TECHNIQUES GIVE THE MONSTER A THREE-DIMENSIONAL APPEARANCE.

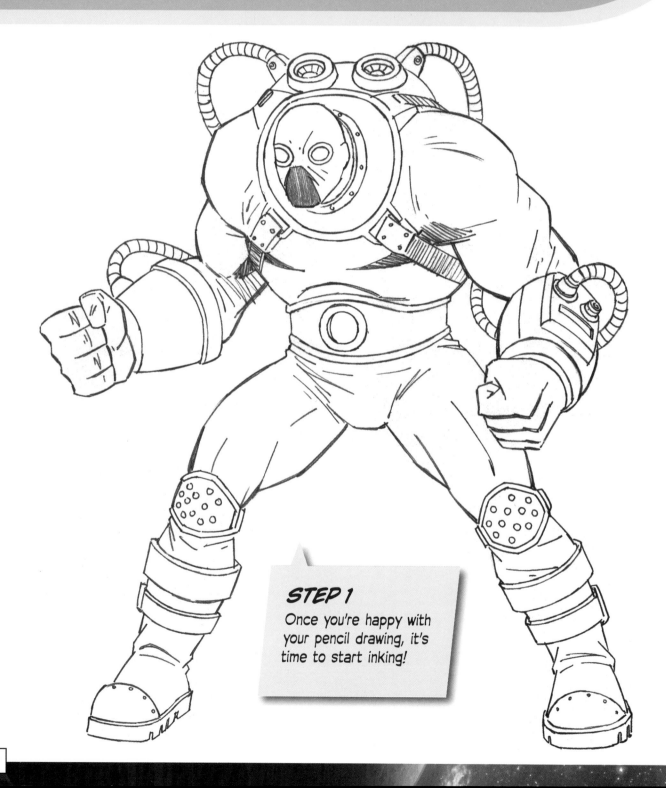

STEP 1
Once you're happy with your pencil drawing, it's time to start inking!

STEP 2

Lots of different line thicknesses are used in this example. In some areas the ink is applied fairly loosely, but in others it is clean and precise. Solid black is used for the mouth area and to define the monster's chest and shoulder muscles.

STEP 3

A light blue followed by a layer of lavender gray is used to create the base color of the suit.

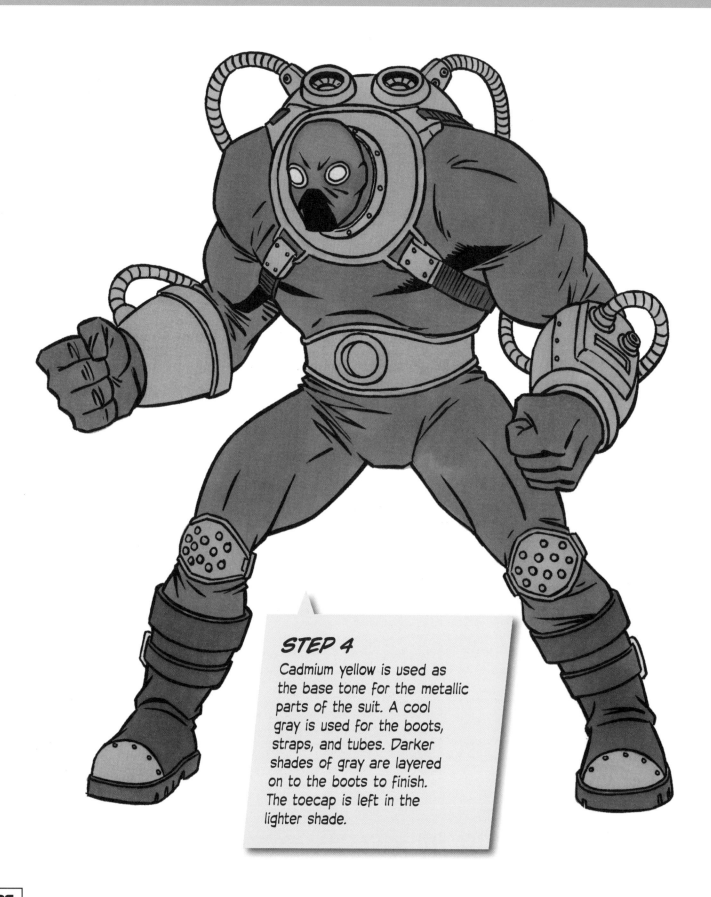

STEP 4

Cadmium yellow is used as the base tone for the metallic parts of the suit. A cool gray is used for the boots, straps, and tubes. Darker shades of gray are layered on to the boots to finish. The toecap is left in the lighter shade.

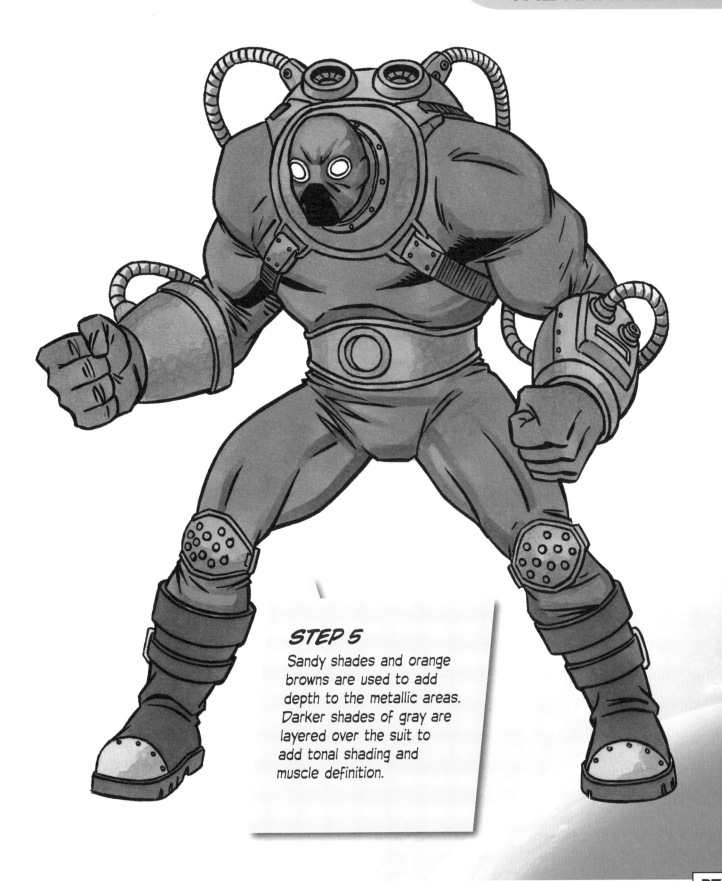

STEP 5

Sandy shades and orange browns are used to add depth to the metallic areas. Darker shades of gray are layered over the suit to add tonal shading and muscle definition.

STEP 6
White highlights are added to his suit and armor and the darker areas of shading are accentuated. The final touch is his glowing red eyes! This guy is ready for action.

THE NEXT LEVEL

NOW THAT YOU'VE LEARNED HOW TO INK AND COLOR YOUR CHARACTER DRAWINGS, HOW ABOUT TACKLING A FULL PAGE OF COMIC-BOOK ART? IT'S REALLY NOT THAT DIFFICULT AND THE SAME PRINCIPLES APPLY.

Here we have a page of comic-book art in pencil. The solid areas of shading are marked in at the pencil stage, so it's just a case of inking faithfully over the pencil lines.

This artwork would work equally well with even more shading. This would create a stronger contrast between the light and dark areas, but it would leave less room for color.

As you follow the step-by-step sequence, you'll see how the areas of ink and color work together in the panels, just as they do when you're coloring an individual figure.

FIG. 1

INKING STYLES FOR PANELS

Some artists like to ink the panel outlines freehand, without the aid of a ruler. This creates a nice contrast between the panel edge and the clean, crisp lines within the panel (Fig. 1). You can also use a loose line style inside the panel for a slightly sketchier finish (Fig. 2).

FIG. 2

THE FINISHED RESULT

INKED PAGE

So here it is, our fully inked comic-book page. When you're creating your own comic, you could choose to keep things simple and leave your artwork in black and white. However the addition of color will really bring your comic-book pages to life.

We have kept the line style clean and precise throughout. Very little shading has been added so that we have plenty of space left in which to apply color.

The solid areas of black create dramatic blocks of dark shading. We will also use layers of color to determine areas of light and shade in the final version.

We used markers to color the page above, but a similar effect could be achieved using watercolors or liquid inks. Plan your color palette before you start to apply any color, and keep it simple!

When coloring your artwork, choose colors that help show what time of day it is. This story is set at night and the light source is the moon. To achieve a moonlit effect, use light blue as your base color on all panels.

In panel 1 we establish that the light source is the moon. On top of the light blue, layers of olive green and cool gray are applied to color the trees.

Pale blue, olive and gray are also used for panels 2, 3, and 4.

The girl's skin tone and hair are colored brightly, making her the focal point.

Cool gray is used to add shading to her skin, hair, and dress.

In the final panel we have allowed moonlit areas of pale blue to show through on the trees and grass. This keeps the tone of the light consistent. The glowing eyes in the forest are left white.

LIGHTING AN IMAGE

IN THE PAST, THE COLOR IN COMIC STRIPS WAS FAIRLY BASIC AND SIMPLE. THE COST OF PRODUCTION AND THE LIMITED TECHNOLOGY MEANT THAT ONLY FLAT COLORS COULD REALISTICALLY BE USED. BUT NOWADAYS COMIC-BOOK COLORING IS INCREASINGLY SOPHISTICATED. THE STYLE OF COLORING THAT YOU CHOOSE WILL AFFECT THE OVERALL FEEL OF YOUR GRAPHIC NOVEL.

LIGHT AND SHADE
This rich coloring molds the image. The character looks sculpted and, with light and shade added, she is almost three-dimensional.

FLAT COLORS
Some artists prefer to work with large areas of flat color. This creates a more stylized effect, because it looks less like the real world.

COLOR AND ATMOSPHERE

Coloring can also create a strong sense of time, place, and mood. Think to yourself: where is the character? What emotion do you want readers to feel?

WARM COLORS

This image has a golden tone that feels warm and positive.

COLD COLORS

These cold blue tones create a sinister, nighttime mood.

PART 2: SUPERHERO COMICS

WHAT MAKES A GREAT COMICS HERO?

It depends who you ask. Most of the superheroes of the Golden Age of Comic Books, from the 1930s to the early 1950s, were essentially wish-fulfilment characters. They had incredible powers, good looks, and plenty of moral fiber!

FLAWED SUPERHEROES

In the 1960s, flawed superheroes became popular. These characters' extraordinary abilities were offset by real-life problems, such as a hostile public, and character defects, such as arrogance. Some heroes saw their powers as a curse.

MODERN-DAY CHARACTERS

In the 21st century, many comic creators have tried to better represent the diversity of people in the modern world. By giving your characters varied backgrounds and interesting flaws and problems, you can make them feel compelling.

HOW TO DRAW

G-FORCE

ARE YOU READY TO DRAW YOUR FIRST SUPERHERO? ROCKET SCIENTIST TODD TRAVIS WAS BUILDING THE WARP DRIVE OF AN EXPERIMENTAL SHIP WHEN THE ENGINE EXPLODED. THE COSMIC ENERGY GAVE HIM THE ABILITY TO CONTROL GRAVITY. NOW HE FIGHTS CRIME ACROSS THE GALAXY!

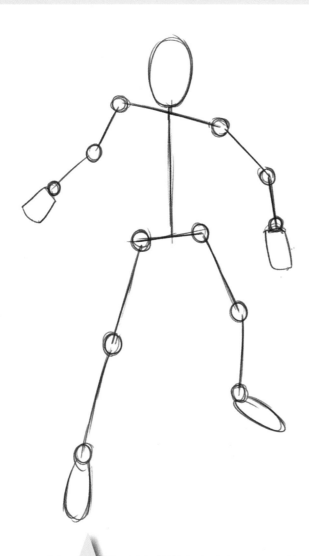

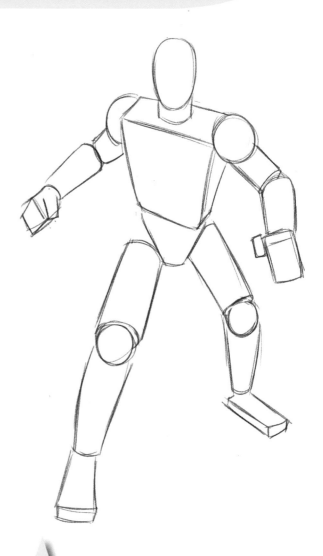

STEP 1
It's important that you get the initial pose and proportions right. Sketch a wireframe showing limbs and joints.

STEP 2
Use basic shapes to build on top of your wireframe. His hips are triangular, and his chest tapers to the waist. The leg that is closest to us looks slightly longer than the trailing leg.

STEP 3

Now you can bulk up the body and outline where the features will go. Sketch in G-Force's leg and arm muscles, and define those in his stomach area. Round off the joints and add details to the hands and feet, including fingers and knuckles.

STEP 4

It's costume time! What is your newly invented character going to look like? G-Force has some high-tech nodes across his chest and on his belt, which help him keep control of his gravity powers. His identity is hidden by a domino mask.

STEP 5

The inking stage is your opportunity to choose the strongest lines in your illustration and bring them out with nice, sharp line work. Keep your hand steady as you outline those muscles. This cosmic hero is bulked-up and brainy so bad guys had better beware!

STEP 6

When you're happy with your character, you can add color. Pick a bold blue and red. Use darker and paler tones for shadows and highlights. Classic superheroes tend to have primary colors—red, blue, and yellow—as their color palette.

CREATING HEROES

IF YOU'RE CREATING YOUR OWN SUPERHERO COMIC, YOU MIGHT WANT TO USE YOUR OWN SUPERHEROES OR SUPERVILLAINS. WHERE CAN YOU FIND INSPIRATION FOR NEW CHARACTERS?

ANIMAL HEROES

One way to devise a new character is to take inspiration from an animal. Many superheroes, such as Batman and Spider-Man, have the characteristics and capabilities of animals.

Magpie is an excellent thief. Like real magpies, she has a love of shiny things, such as priceless jewels!

NATURE HEROES

You can take your starting point from other aspects of nature, such as clouds, rainbows, volcanoes, or plants.

Tanglevine's body is covered in tough, thorny armor. He can use the vines sprouting from his back to entangle his enemies.

STORYBOOK HEROES

Some comic characters are inspired by other fictional characters, such as the mythical god Thor or Robin Hood.

This savage superhero, the Scarlet Hood, is inspired by the story of Red Riding Hood. Like the heroine of that story, she wears a long red cloak. She also has the claws of a big, bad wolf!

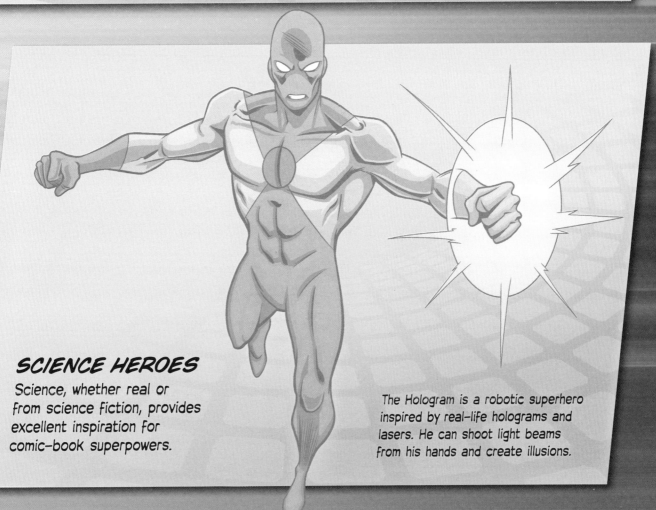

SCIENCE HEROES

Science, whether real or from science fiction, provides excellent inspiration for comic-book superpowers.

The Hologram is a robotic superhero inspired by real-life holograms and lasers. He can shoot light beams from his hands and create illusions.

HOW TO DRAW
SILVER SORCERESS

THIS FEISTY SUPERHEROINE IS CONSTRUCTED USING THE SAME BASIC TECHNIQUES AS OUR MALE HERO. SHE IS SHOWN WITH TELEKINETIC ENERGY GLOWING AROUND HER HANDS.

STEP 1
Start by drawing the basic stick figure. Female characters have smaller waists and narrower shoulders than males.

STEP 2
Draw an outline around the shapes to flesh out your figure. Draw the hands and map out the proportions of the face.

STEP 3

Add in the facial features, hair, and clothing.

STEP 4

Erase your working lines and add final details. Draw the energy blasts she has conjured from the palms of her hands. She's ready for action!

STEP 5
Ink your character with clean, sharp lines.

STEP 6
Choose colors for your character's costume that will make your character stand out.

STYLES OF COMIC ART

THERE'S MORE THAN ONE WAY TO DRAW A COMIC CHARACTER! DOC TWILIGHT HAS THE ABILITY TO CONTROL LIGHT AND DARKNESS... AND HERE WE'VE DRAWN HIM WITH FOUR DIFFERENT APPROACHES.

MODERN SUPERHERO ART

Let's start with a modern take on our hero. Notice how the line work is light on the Doc's face, but it's heavier on his body. There are few large areas of ink. His face is very moody— he's almost grimacing!

ALL-ACTION STYLE

This "retro" art style harks back to the energetic line work of famous comic artist Jack Kirby. The lines on Doc Twilight's face and body are more angular—many of them are shaped like zigzags.

ANIMATED STYLE

In this "animated" style, the line work is much simpler. The detail is reduced in favor of clean, sweeping lines, but the proportions remain realistic. The shadows are turned into flat blocks of black ink.

NOIR STYLE

Noir is the French word for black. It's a style of artwork that tends to be used for stories about crime or the supernatural. It has large areas of shadow in place of fine details, with a strong contrast between colors.

HOW TO DRAW
THE BLUE COMET

THIS CHARACTER IS DRAWN IN A DIFFERENT ART STYLE. YOU MAY BE FAMILIAR WITH THIS SLICK, STYLIZED LOOK FROM ANIMATED SUPERHERO PROGRAMS ON TV.

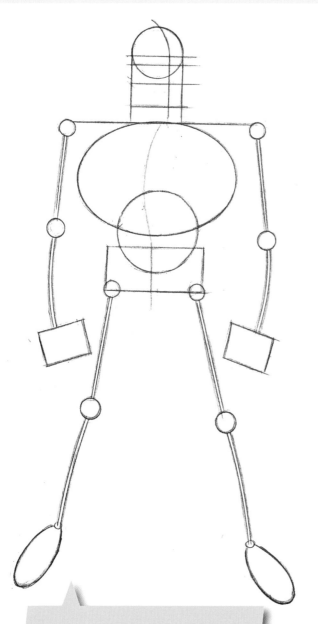

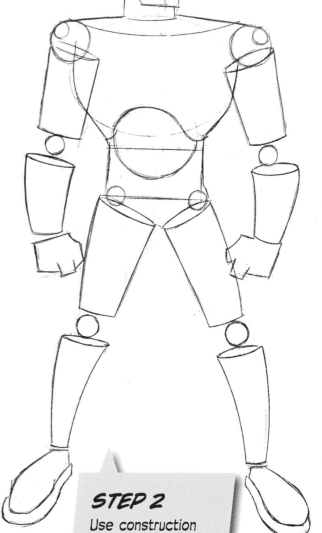

STEP 1
Start with some simple shapes fixed to a basic frame.

STEP 2
Use construction shapes to flesh him out. He has to look dramatic even when standing still.

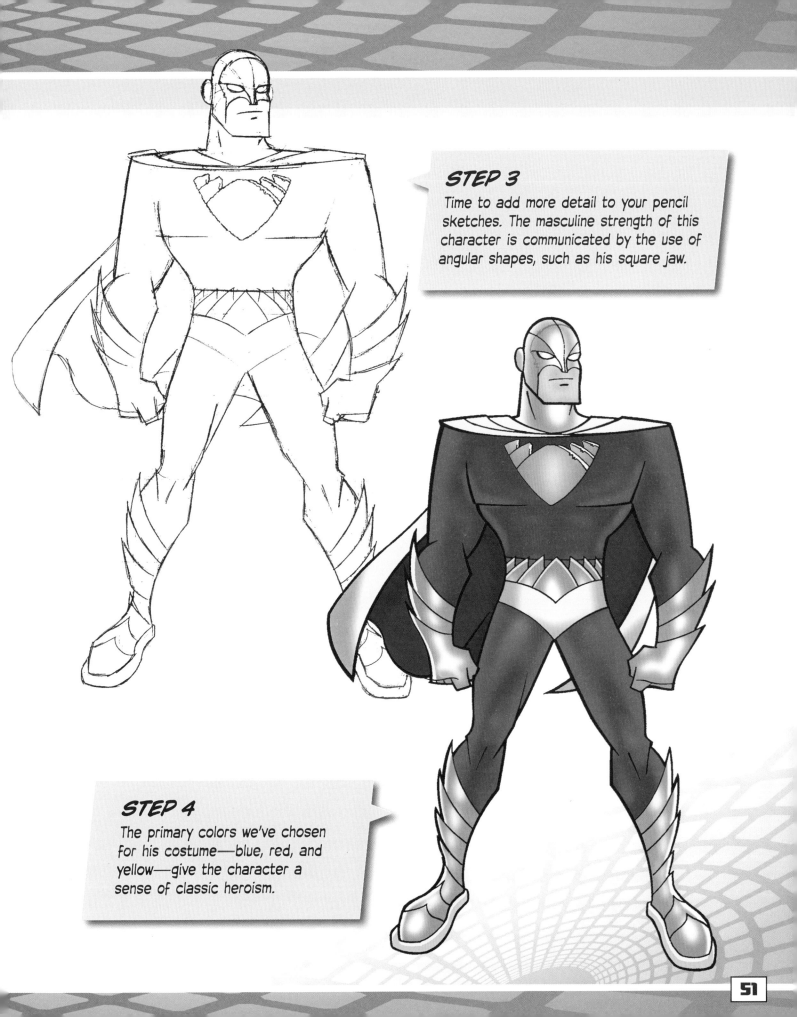

STEP 3

Time to add more detail to your pencil sketches. The masculine strength of this character is communicated by the use of angular shapes, such as his square jaw.

STEP 4

The primary colors we've chosen for his costume—blue, red, and yellow—give the character a sense of classic heroism.

HOW TO DRAW
ROCKET GIRL

DON'T BE FOOLED INTO THINKING THAT "ANIMATED" STYLE SUPERHERO ART IS SUPER-EASY! YOU STILL NEED TO THINK ABOUT HOW THE SHAPES THAT MAKE UP THE BODY FIT TOGETHER, AND FOLLOW THE SAME STEPS OF PENCILING, INKING, AND COLORING.

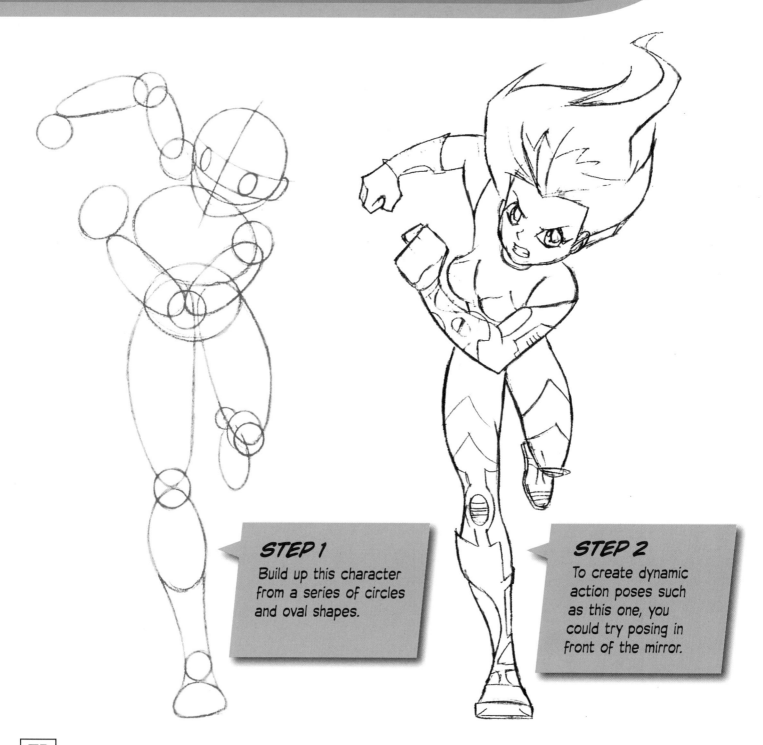

STEP 1
Build up this character from a series of circles and oval shapes.

STEP 2
To create dynamic action poses such as this one, you could try posing in front of the mirror.

STEP 3

Use thin lines for detail and a thicker line of ink around the outside of the figure. This will make her "pop out" of the page.

STEP 4

The colors you choose will put across the character's personality. Colors like purple and green suggest that a hero is an unpredictable wild card.

MAKE A MONSTER

EVERYONE LOVES A GOOD BAD GUY! A STRONG VILLAIN WILL BE ESSENTIAL FOR CREATING DRAMA IN YOUR GRAPHIC NOVEL. WHEN YOU CREATE YOUR HERO'S ENEMY, ASK YOURSELF: WHAT IS HIS MOTIVATION? DOES HE CRAVE MONEY OR POWER? IS HE EVIL, CRAZY, OR JUST MISGUIDED? WHAT ARE HIS POWERS AND ABILITIES? FOR A VILLAIN TO RISE UP THE RANKS, HE MUST BE A REAL THREAT TO YOUR HERO. LET YOUR IMAGINATION RUN WILD!

SUPERNATURAL THREAT

Supernatural themes in comic books offer great opportunities to create ghoulish characters. Your villain could be a crazed creature who has risen from the grave, seeking revenge. He could also be a dark force from another dimension, capable of bending the laws of physics.

VAMPIRE

The undead, especially vampires, are a popular choice for writers of horror comics. Vampire abilities include superhuman strength, enhanced speed, and the ability to regenerate. These powers make them very tricky opponents to defeat.

CRAZED MAGICIAN

Your villain could be an evil magician with uncanny powers. Such an illusionist could create many mind-bending obstacles for your hero. His skills might include telepathy, teleportation, energy blasts, and the creation of protective force fields.

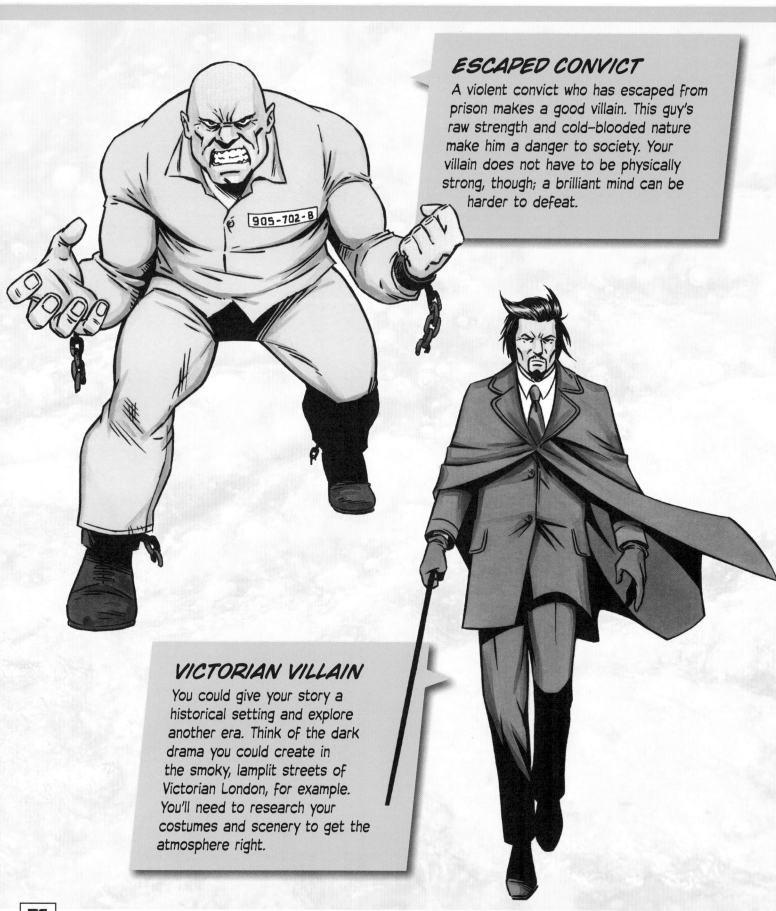

ESCAPED CONVICT

A violent convict who has escaped from prison makes a good villain. This guy's raw strength and cold-blooded nature make him a danger to society. Your villain does not have to be physically strong, though; a brilliant mind can be harder to defeat.

VICTORIAN VILLAIN

You could give your story a historical setting and explore another era. Think of the dark drama you could create in the smoky, lamplit streets of Victorian London, for example. You'll need to research your costumes and scenery to get the atmosphere right.

SINISTER CLOWN

Clowns, puppets, and mannequins are often used to great dramatic effect in tales of suspense and horror. Heavy makeup and oversized, colorful costumes mask the true emotions and intentions of the performer, which can be unnerving. The brightly painted, jolly face of a clown can suddenly take on a sinister appearance when it masks the face of a fiend.

MAD SCIENTIST

Crazy professors spend their time mixing lethal chemicals, designing deadly weapons or creating superhuman creatures. They can be fun to build into your story. What will your mad scientist unleash upon an unsuspecting world?

HOW TO DRAW
THE CONVICT

FOLLOW THE SAME STEPS FOR DRAWING VILLAINS AS YOU DID FOR HEROES, BUT WHILE HEROES APPEAR TALL AND NOBLE, VILLAINS MAKE THREATENING AND AGGRESSIVE POSES.

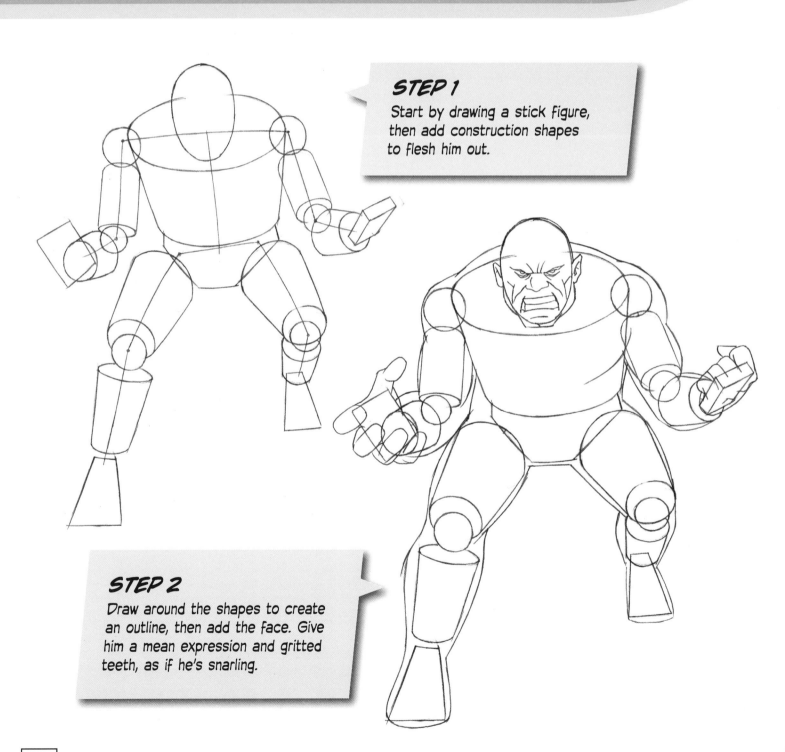

STEP 1
Start by drawing a stick figure, then add construction shapes to flesh him out.

STEP 2
Draw around the shapes to create an outline, then add the face. Give him a mean expression and gritted teeth, as if he's snarling.

STEP 3

Remove your working lines and clean up your pencil drawing. Start adding detail, such as the convict's standard-issue prison uniform.

905-702-8

STEP 4

Finish your pencil drawing by adding broken chains and shackles. Add some shading, blocking in the areas that will be inked solidly in black.

905-702-8

STEP 5
Carefully following your pencil lines, ink your drawing to give it more power and impact.

905-702-B

STEP 6
Coloring this character is very simple as you only need three colors; peach for the skin tones, blue for the uniform, and dark gray for the chains and boots.

HOW TO DRAW
PROFESSOR VILE

THIS ARCHETYPAL MAD SCIENTIST IS SKINNY RATHER THAN MUSCULAR, BUT HE STILL STRIKES AN UNSETTLING POSE, SHOWING OFF WHAT IS SURE TO BE A DEADLY FORMULA FROM HIS LAB OF HORRORS.

STEP 1
Start to draw the figure using a stick frame. Add construction shapes to the frame.

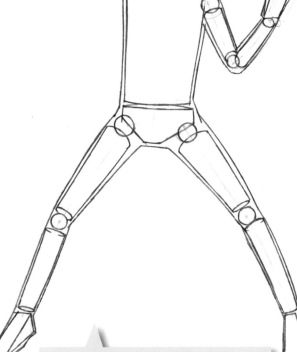

STEP 2
Draw the face and hair. Give this character an exaggerated expression.

STEP 3

Clean up your pencil work and draw his clothing. We've chosen a classic lab coat for this nutty professor. Draw the bubbling potion he is holding.

STEP 4

Finalize your pencil drawing by adding shading, to prepare it for inking.

STEP 6

Time to add color! Shades of light gray and blue have been used for the lab coat, shirt, and hair. A darker gray has been applied to the pants and shoes. These simple colors really make the bright green potion and scientist's goggles pop out of the page!

HOW TO DRAW

THE VOLCANOID

IT'S TIME TO UNLEASH A BIG-LEAGUE SUPERVILLAIN! THE VOLCANOID IS INSPIRED BY REAL-LIFE VOLCANOES. HE HAS A ROCKY HIDE AND CAN SHOOT DEADLY BLASTS OF MOLTEN LAVA. HE HAS A HEAVY, BULKY "BRUISER" BUILD AND AN UNUSUAL, ROCKY SKIN TEXTURE.

STEP 1

Start with an oversized wireframe. Make its head small, but exaggerate the size of its feet and hands.

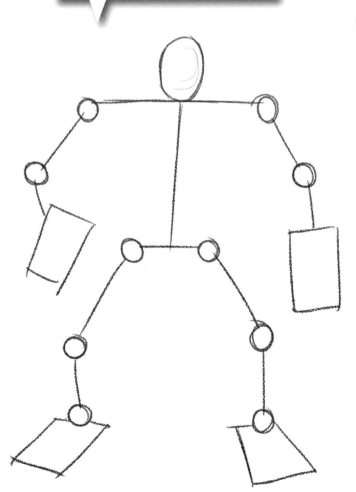

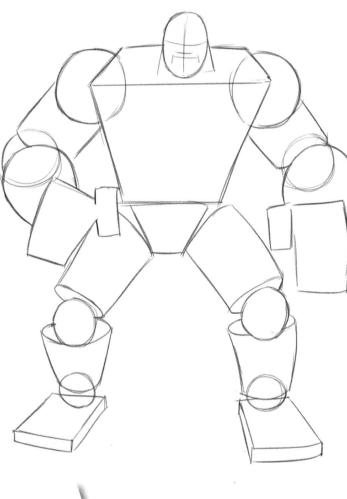

STEP 2

Build on the frame using basic shapes. Begin to fill out the figure, building it up around the shoulders, forearms, and lower legs. Its upper torso should be broad, narrowing at the waist.

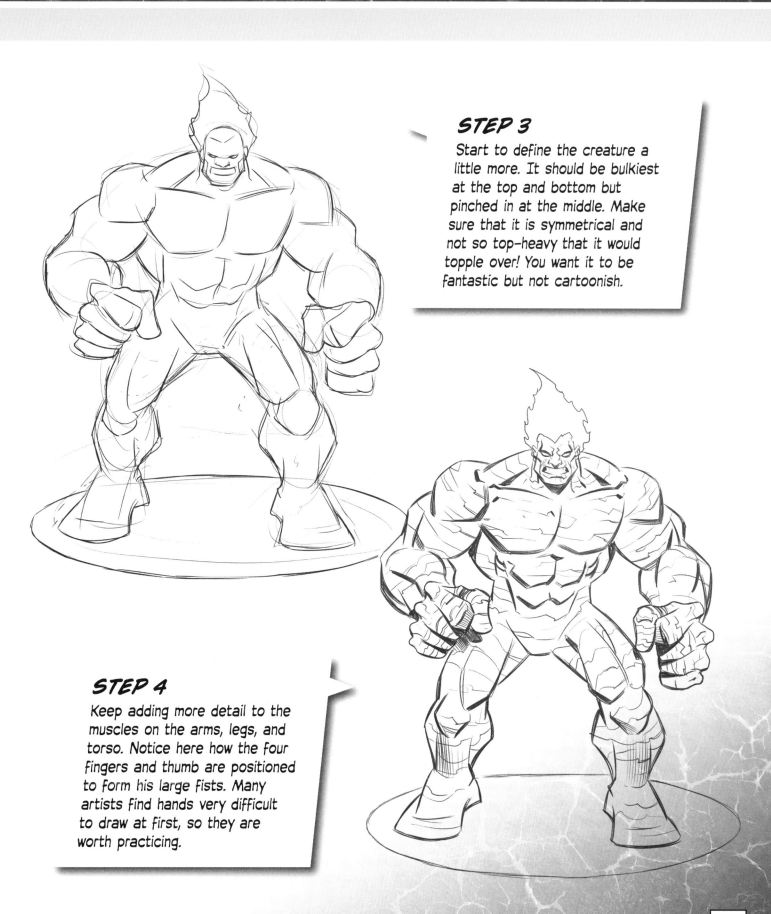

STEP 3

Start to define the creature a little more. It should be bulkiest at the top and bottom but pinched in at the middle. Make sure that it is symmetrical and not so top-heavy that it would topple over! You want it to be fantastic but not cartoonish.

STEP 4

Keep adding more detail to the muscles on the arms, legs, and torso. Notice here how the four fingers and thumb are positioned to form his large fists. Many artists find hands very difficult to draw at first, so they are worth practicing.

STEP 5

Work up the hair, which is flamelike, in keeping with the volcanic theme of the character. It also reminds your reader of the otherworldly, nonhuman traits of this monster. He has no costume since he is a creature of the rocks and earth.

STEP 6

The purple hues we have chosen for the Volcanoid's skin don't look like normal rock, but they are more eye–catching than gray tones. Notice how the molten lava glows through the orange cracks in his skin texture. His hair, eyes, and mouth are all glowing!

HOW TO DRAW
THE BARBARIC BRUTE

WHY NOT EXPERIMENT WITH DIFFERENT ART STYLES? THE NEXT TWO VILLAINS HAVE A SLICK, STYLIZED LOOK. THE STREAMLINED DESIGN IS LIKE THAT USED IN TV SUPERHERO ANIMATIONS.

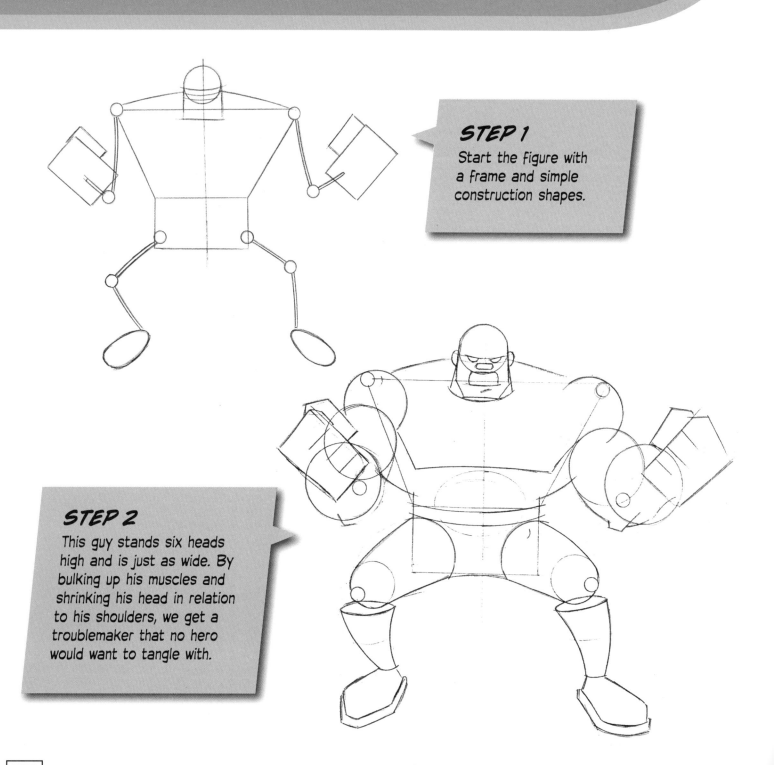

STEP 1
Start the figure with a frame and simple construction shapes.

STEP 2
This guy stands six heads high and is just as wide. By bulking up his muscles and shrinking his head in relation to his shoulders, we get a troublemaker that no hero would want to tangle with.

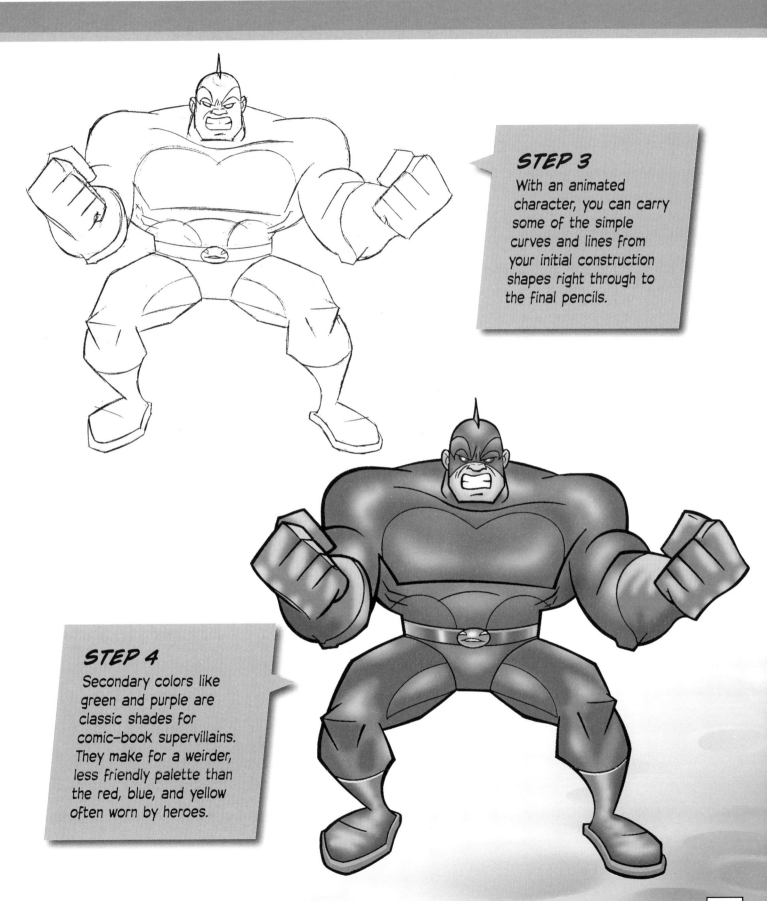

STEP 3
With an animated character, you can carry some of the simple curves and lines from your initial construction shapes right through to the final pencils.

STEP 4
Secondary colors like green and purple are classic shades for comic-book supervillains. They make for a weirder, less friendly palette than the red, blue, and yellow often worn by heroes.

HOW TO DRAW

THE SILENT ASSASSIN

THIS FEMALE CHARACTER ALSO HAS THE CLEAN, SIMPLE LINES OF AN ANIMATED CHARACTER. HOWEVER, RATHER THAN BEING BULKY AND SQUAT, SHE IS TALL AND ELEGANT.

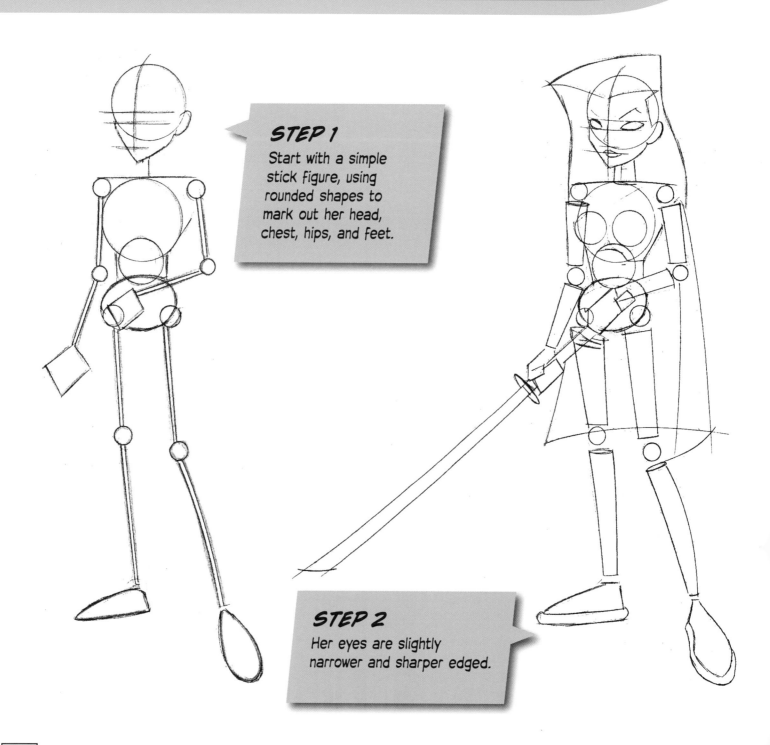

STEP 1

Start with a simple stick figure, using rounded shapes to mark out her head, chest, hips, and feet.

STEP 2

Her eyes are slightly narrower and sharper edged.

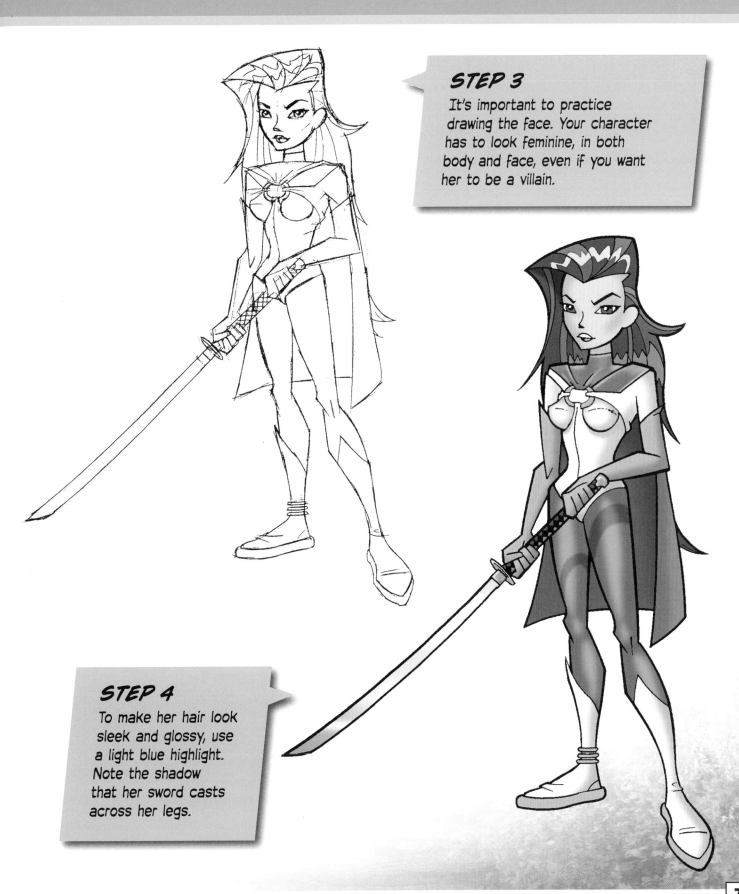

STEP 3

It's important to practice drawing the face. Your character has to look feminine, in both body and face, even if you want her to be a villain.

STEP 4

To make her hair look sleek and glossy, use a light blue highlight. Note the shadow that her sword casts across her legs.

DEADLY DEMON

Does your villain serve a more powerful master? Perhaps he follows the orders of a demon, the very embodiment of evil.

UNDERWORLD BOSS

Criminal bosses are ruthless, powerful characters. Gangsters make great archvillains and are characters we love to hate.

WICKED WARLORD
A crazy military mastermind with evil ambitions could command the evil forces in your story.

GRAND HIGH NINJA
A super-powered martial artist is a formidable opponent for any hero.

ACTION POSES

EXAGGERATION

IN SUPERHERO COMICS, CHARACTERS' MOVEMENTS TEND TO BE LARGER THAN LIFE. READERS WANT TO SEE THEIR HEROES IN CONSTANT ACTION! ARTISTS USE VARIOUS TRICKS TO TAKE A REALISTIC MOVEMENT AND EXAGGERATE IT TO INCREASE ITS VISUAL IMPACT.

REALISTIC RUNNING

When captured in a drawing, realistic running can look surprisingly slow and stately. The limbs of an actual runner swing only so much, and the body is fairly upright.

DYNAMIC RUNNING

In this dynamic image, the character's arms and legs are flung forward and backward, with the body at an extreme angle. The leading hand is very near to us, and the trailing foot seems far away.

REALISTIC PUNCH

A real boxer would be balanced when he throws a punch, keeping his body upright and his feet grounded for maximum stability. But that doesn't look so exciting when you draw it...

DYNAMIC PUNCH

Instead, a superhero artist relaxes that approach and shifts the body and arms. The punching arm is almost fully extended, while the rear arm is less defensive. Motion lines show power and speed.

RUNNING: FRONT VIEW

Let's get moving! Here are some running poses viewed from the front. The second version (Fig. 2) is more dynamic. You can really feel the action. It looks like the figure could leap off the page toward you! Try to choose poses that feel high-powered and energetic. These will make your graphic novel feel action-packed.

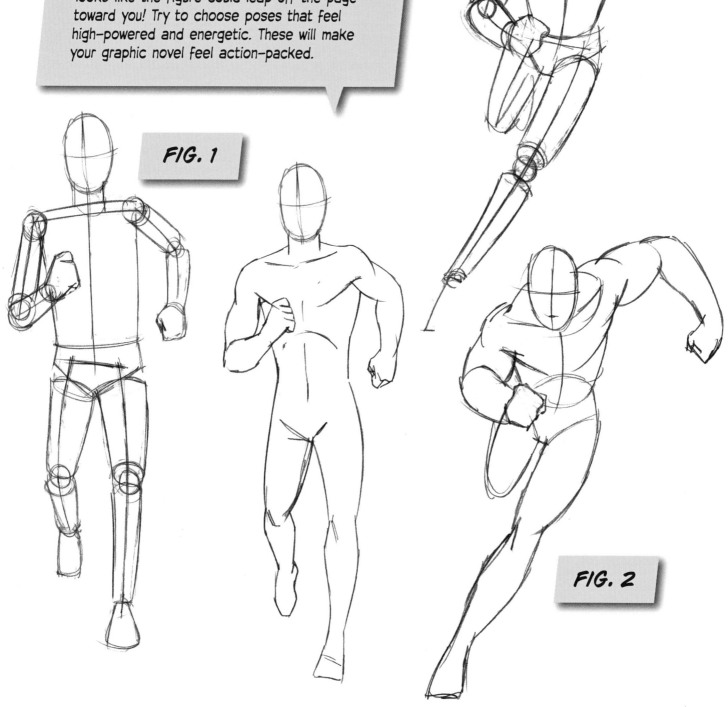

FIG. 1

FIG. 2

RUNNING: SIDE VIEW

Look at the images of two different side-view running poses below. Which one do you find more interesting? The figure in a casual running pose on the left (Fig. 3) or the figure on the right who looks like he's about to take off (Fig. 4)? No contest! Sometimes it helps to start off with a more boring pose then exaggerate the action you're drawing gradually, in stages, until you end up with a really exciting pose.

FIG. 3

FIG. 4

ACTION POSES

RUNNING

HERE'S A STEP-BY-STEP GUIDE TO DRAWING, INKING, AND COLORING A RUNNING CHARACTER. THE MAIN THING ABOUT THIS POSE IS THAT IT'S NOT BALANCED. IF YOU TRIED TO STAND LIKE THIS YOURSELF, YOU WOULD FALL OVER. THAT IMBALANCE HELPS GIVE THE IMPRESSION OF MOVEMENT.

STEP 1
Draw the character's head, chest, and pelvis first. You are drawing her body from the side but with it leaning forward so the body parts follow a diagonal line. Now add the limbs.

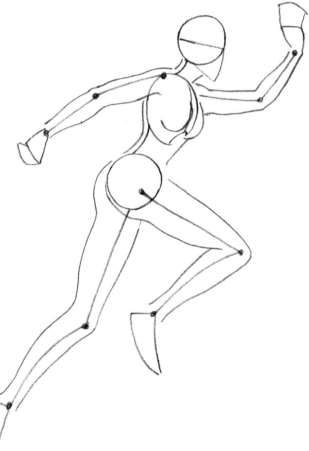

STEP 2
Draw the outline shape of her flesh and muscle. Notice how there are strong curves in the shape at the backs of the legs to show her strong muscles.

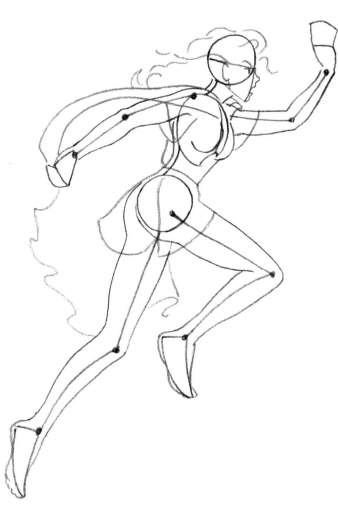

STEP 3

Add some basic lines for her tunic and cloak. Add the main features of the face and some of the curves of the hair. Work on the shape of the feet.

STEP 4

Give the clothing more detail. Notice the square-shaped neck of the tunic. Draw some lines along the bottom of the skirt and cloak to show the folds. Work on the hands and feet. She is wearing sandals, so you'll still be able to see her toes in the final picture.

STEP 5

Once you're happy with your drawing, go over your pencil lines in ink. Now add some shading to the hair to give it more depth.

STEP 6

Leave the ink to dry, then erase all your remaining pencil guidelines.

STEP 7

Now you can add some color to your picture. We've given her auburn hair and a green tunic. Notice how dark the inside of the cloak is where it is in shadow.

ACTION POSES
IN COMBAT

IF YOU PLAN TO SHOW YOUR HEROES AND VILLAINS IN CONFLICT, YOU'LL NEED TO LEARN HOW TO DRAW COMBAT POSES.

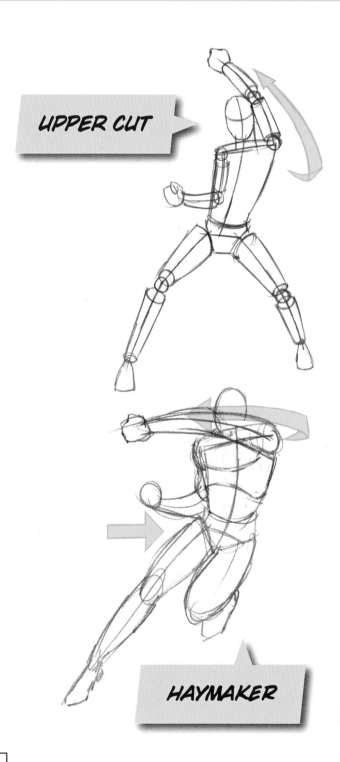

UPPER CUT

DIVING PUNCH

HAYMAKER

PUNCHING
To draw a really convincing punch, you have to consider the flow and direction of the action. Look at the three different examples on this page. Arrows have been added to show the flow of action through the body.

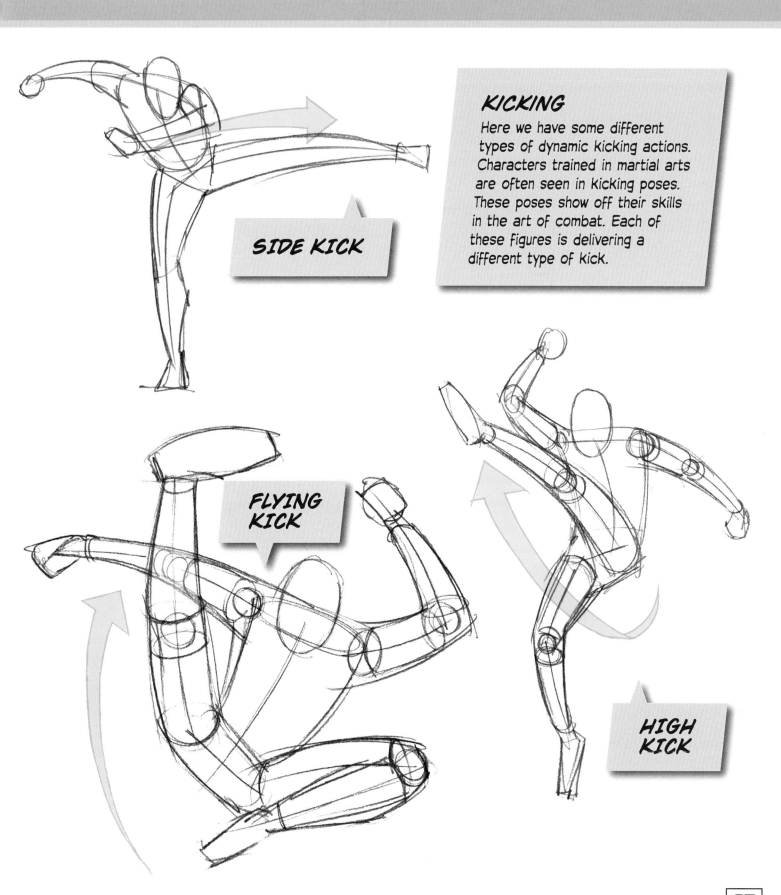

KICKING

Here we have some different types of dynamic kicking actions. Characters trained in martial arts are often seen in kicking poses. These poses show off their skills in the art of combat. Each of these figures is delivering a different type of kick.

SIDE KICK

FLYING KICK

HIGH KICK

ACTION POSES

FIGHTING HERO

THIS HERO HAS HIS RIGHT HAND PULLED BACK,
READY TO DELIVER A WALL-SMASHING PUNCH.

STEP 1
Start by creating
the loose, skeletal
stick figure.

STEP 2
Flesh out the
figure using the
construction shapes.

STEP 3
Now begin to develop the outer form
of the figure, adding basic muscle
detail. At this stage you should keep
your pencil sketch loose and light.

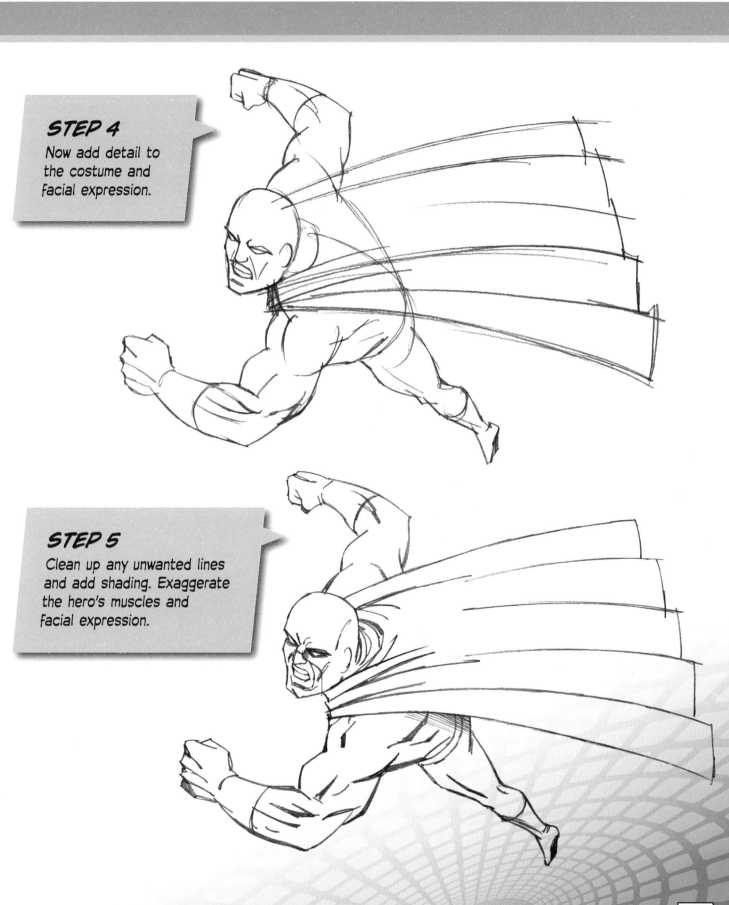

STEP 4
Now add detail to the costume and facial expression.

STEP 5
Clean up any unwanted lines and add shading. Exaggerate the hero's muscles and facial expression.

STEP 7

The hero's cape billows out behind him as he lunges forward. This gives the image a real sense of movement. Individually shade each fold of the cape to make it look three-dimensional.

ACTION POSES

INTO THE AIR

TO CREATE STRONG ACTION POSES, YOU MUST FEEL THE ACTION. DON'T DRAW TOO RIGIDLY AT FIRST OR YOU WILL END UP WITH A STIFF POSE. START WITH A SERIES OF LOOSE SKETCHES. IT DOESN'T MATTER IF YOU DON'T PRODUCE A PERFECT DRAWING RIGHT AWAY.

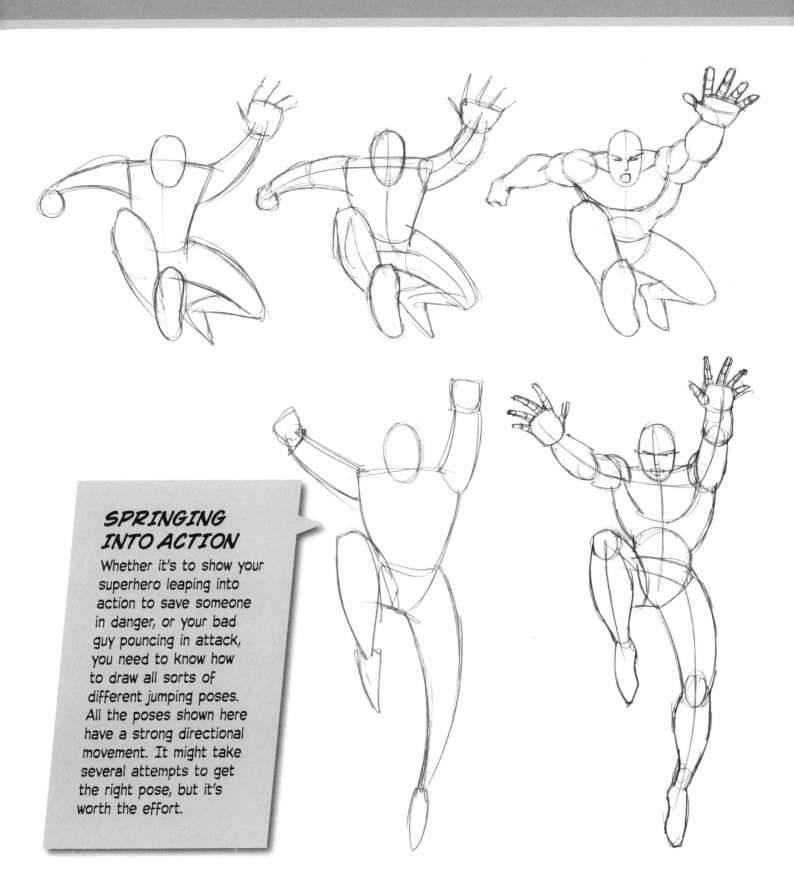

SPRINGING INTO ACTION

Whether it's to show your superhero leaping into action to save someone in danger, or your bad guy pouncing in attack, you need to know how to draw all sorts of different jumping poses. All the poses shown here have a strong directional movement. It might take several attempts to get the right pose, but it's worth the effort.

ACTION POSES
SWORD AND SPEED

HERE WE HAVE A SERIES OF ACTION POSES SHOWING USE OF A WEAPON, IN THIS CASE A SWORD. THINK ABOUT THE DIRECTION OF THE ACTION, THEN MAKE YOUR CHARACTER'S BODY FOLLOW IT.

SHOWING SPEED

How can you show that something is happening quickly when your images are static? The answer is speed lines. These are a great way of conveying not just rapid movement, but also intensity and power.

Radial speed lines give a feeling of forward or backward movement. Speed lines can also be horizontal, angular, or vertical (see below).

HORIZONTAL

AT AN ANGLE (FOLLOW THE LINES OF PERSPECTIVE)

VERTICAL

FLOWING MOVEMENT

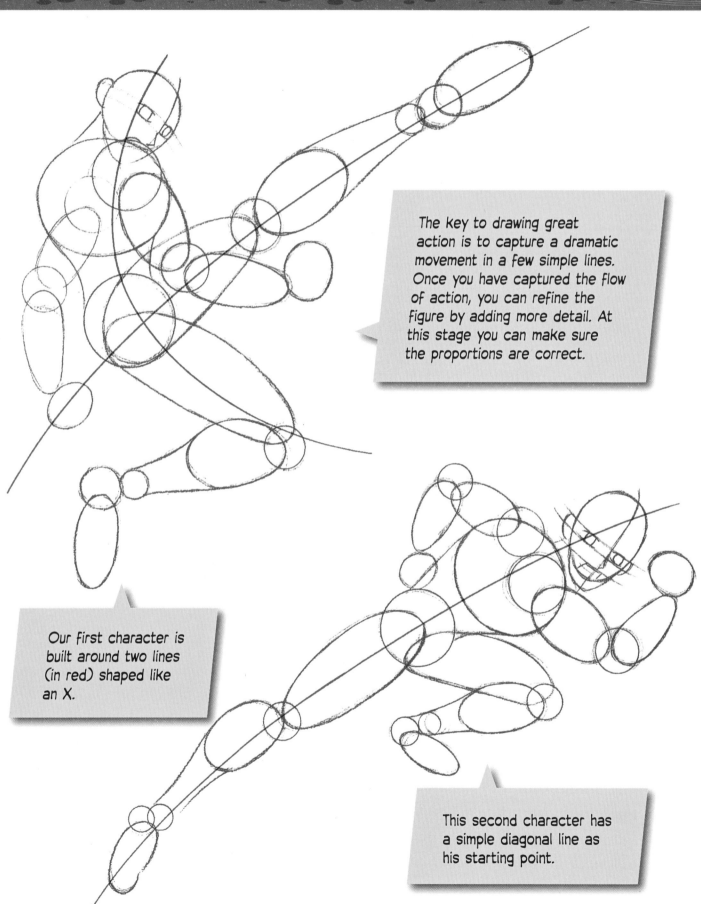

The key to drawing great action is to capture a dramatic movement in a few simple lines. Once you have captured the flow of action, you can refine the figure by adding more detail. At this stage you can make sure the proportions are correct.

Our first character is built around two lines (in red) shaped like an X.

This second character has a simple diagonal line as his starting point.

Capes and hair can play an important role in creating a sense of flowing, directional movement.

FLYING HEROINE

SUPERHERO CHARACTERS SHOULD LOOK LIKE THEY
ARE IN DYNAMIC MOTION AS THEY FLY.

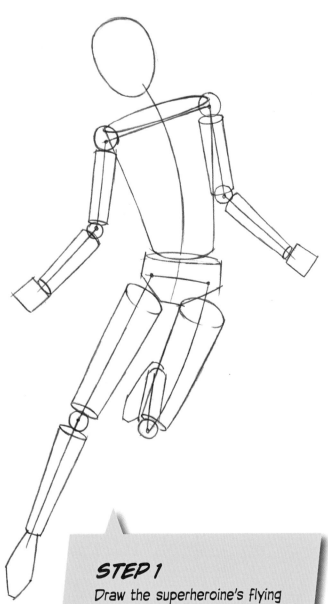

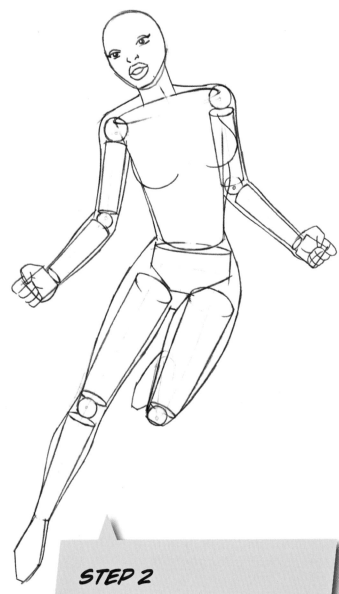

STEP 1
Draw the superheroine's flying
pose using a stick figure,
then build on it with the basic
construction shapes.

STEP 2
Add the facial features and define
the figure by smoothing out the
construction shapes. When you
are happy with how it looks, draw
an outline around the shapes.

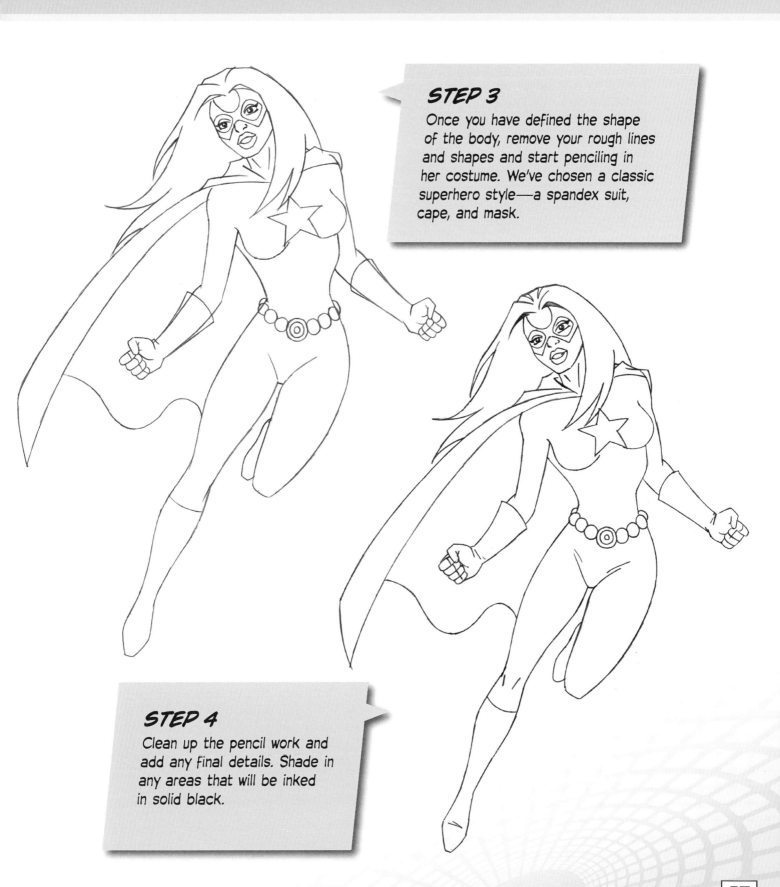

STEP 3

Once you have defined the shape of the body, remove your rough lines and shapes and start penciling in her costume. We've chosen a classic superhero style—a spandex suit, cape, and mask.

STEP 4

Clean up the pencil work and add any final details. Shade in any areas that will be inked in solid black.

STEP 5
Now carefully ink over your pencil work to make your drawing bolder.

STEP 6

Choose a color scheme that complements the character, using a palette that's pleasing to the eye. We have chosen a simple two-color scheme of red and yellow, but there are endless possibilities! Try adapting the colors and suit design to create your own superheroine!

HOW TO DRAW

AN ACTION SCENE

ONCE YOU HAVE PRACTICED DRAWING YOUR CHARACTERS INDIVIDUALLY IN VARIOUS POSES, TRY PITTING THEM AGAINST EACH OTHER IN A DYNAMIC "SPLASH" PANEL. FOLLOW EACH STEP CAREFULLY, AND THE FINAL IMAGE WILL COME TOGETHER PERFECTLY!

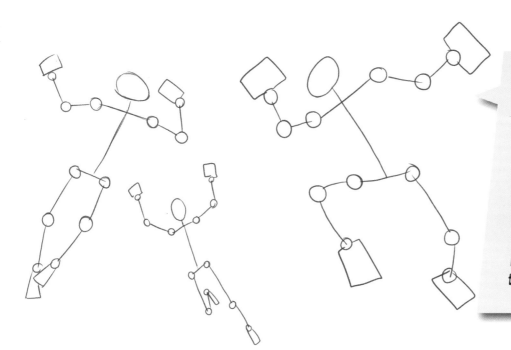

STEP 1

Here, three characters are caught up in an aerial battle. The largest character is the hefty Volcanoid. The superheroine Victory is smaller than G-Force, because she is further away from the viewer.

STEP 2

The outstretched arms of each of the combatants shows they are balanced and poised, either on the floating platform or in midair, ready to strike. Lightly sketch in the buildings behind them, making sure they look three-dimensional and to scale.

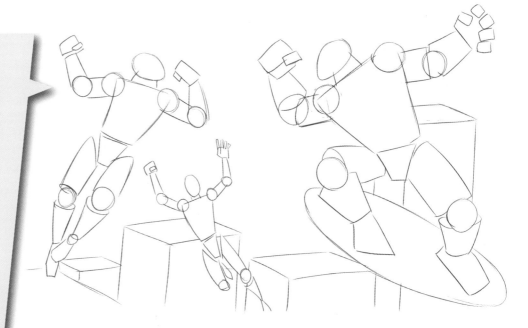

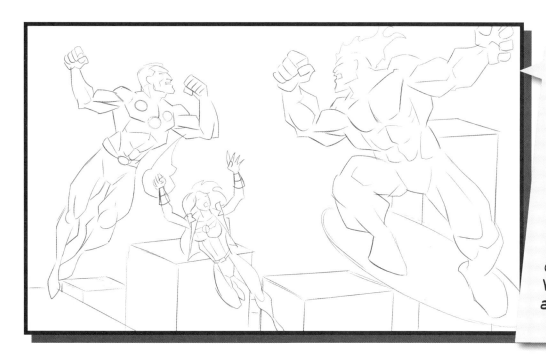

STEP 3

Now flesh out each of your characters. Plan the basic positioning of facial features, and sketch in their muscles and costume elements. Where is each character looking? What are they about to do?

STEP 4

As you ink the image, pay special attention to your characters' faces. Use a ruler to add details to the buildings. Work in some blocks of shading on G-Force's hair, Victory's costume, and the building behind the Volcanoid.

PART 3: SCI-FI COMICS

NEW WORLDS

Unlike superhero comics, set in stylized versions of modern cities, sci-fi stories are set in places drawn entirely from an artist's imagination. That means creating new landscapes, new cities, and new technologies... such as spaceships!

ALIEN ANATOMY

Science fiction artists face the challenge of working with characters with nonhuman proportions, such as robots and aliens. The key to doing this successfully is to pay attention to the basic shapes from which your characters are built.

COSMIC COLLECTION

You may find it helpful to put together a collection of interesting images that you can use as sci-fi inspiration. It could include unusual fashions, strange-looking animals, or cool tech.

HOW TO DRAW

A SPACE PIRATE

CAPTAIN XARA QUINN USED TO WORK FOR THE INTERGALACTIC POLICE, BUT SHE BECAME ANGRY WITH THE CORRUPTION SHE SAW. NOW SHE'S GOING IT ALONE AND KNOWS THERE'S NO SUCH THING AS GOOD GUYS AND BAD GUYS: IT'S EVERY WOMAN FOR HERSELF!

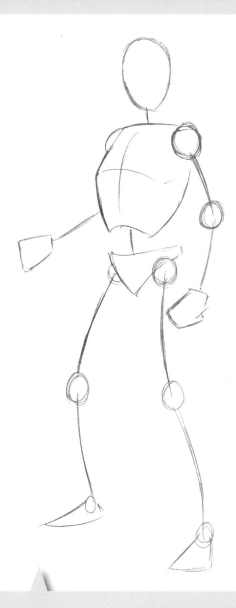

STEP 1
First, you should sketch a wireframe showing how you want Xara to stand. Get the proportions right at this stage.

STEP 2
Flesh out the wireframe with the basic shapes for legs and arms. Add the outline of Xara's military coat and boots. Sketch a cross on her face to get the features in the right place.

STEP 3

In true pirate fashion, Xara has an eyepatch—but hers is a futuristic, cybernetic scanner. Sketch her short, funky hair. Add armored shoulder and knee pads and studded gloves. Her hoop earrings are another nod to old-world pirates.

STEP 4

Work up the details of her outfit, such as her utility belt and thigh cuff. Add shadows underneath her coat. A few delicate lines here and there show the folds of her clothes and boots. Finish the features of her face, keeping her tough but feminine.

STEP 5

Now you can begin to go over your final lines with ink. Erase any guidelines that are still visible. Use a fine pen so that you can draw small details, such as her gloves and buttons. She's a punk pirate, ready for action!

STEP 6

Think carefully about your color scheme. Xara's coat and boots are reminiscent of traditional pirates, but her green spiky hair feels modern or even futuristic. Notice how the shading on her coat uses darker tones of the basic colors.

HOW TO DRAW
A CYBORG

YOU CAN REALLY GO WILD WITH THE DESIGN OF SCIENCE FICTION CHARACTERS. HOWEVER, IF YOU WANT YOUR READERS TO RELATE TO THESE HEROES, THEY MUST STILL LOOK RECOGNIZABLY HUMAN.

STEP 1

Construct the pose by drawing a stick figure and then add construction shapes. The cyborg has both feet firmly planted on the ground in this front-on pose.

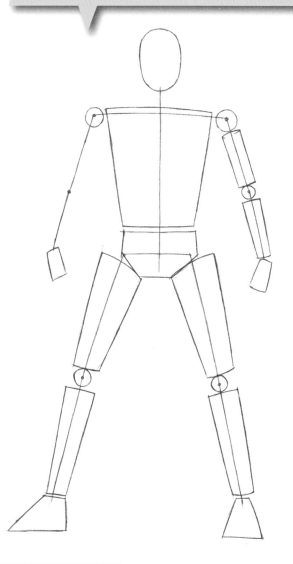

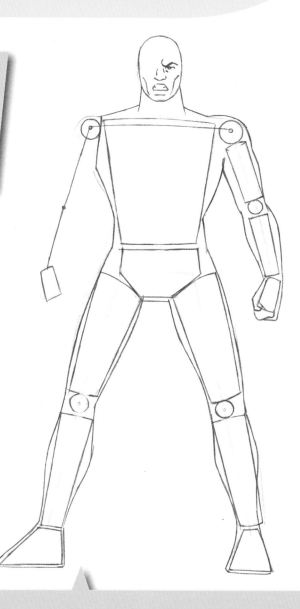

STEP 2

Using the construction shapes as a base, begin to define the muscle structure of this well-built hero. Start penciling in the face.

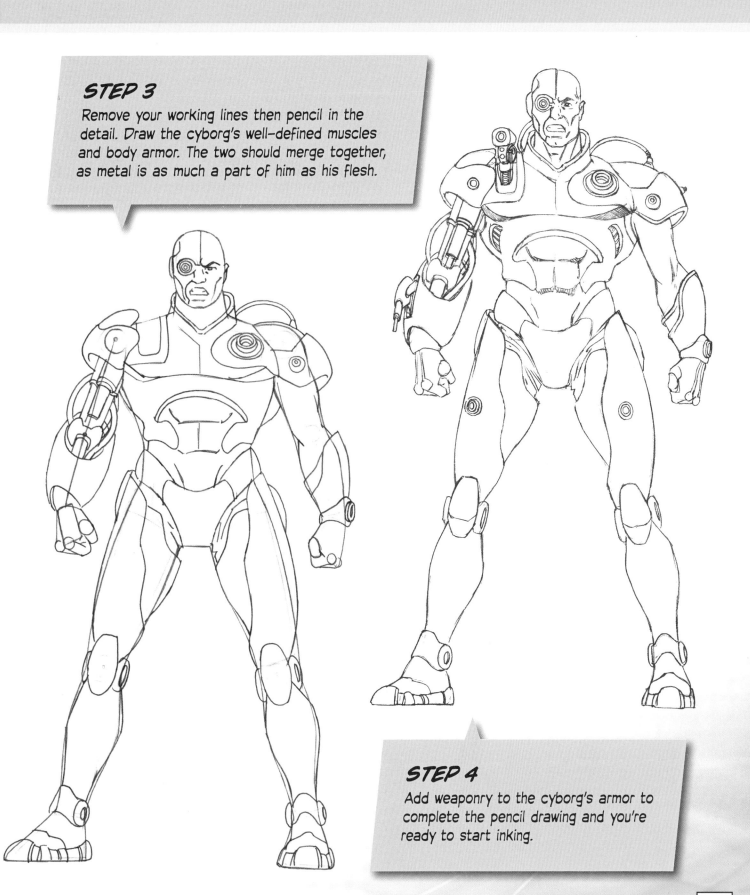

STEP 3

Remove your working lines then pencil in the detail. Draw the cyborg's well-defined muscles and body armor. The two should merge together, as metal is as much a part of him as his flesh.

STEP 4

Add weaponry to the cyborg's armor to complete the pencil drawing and you're ready to start inking.

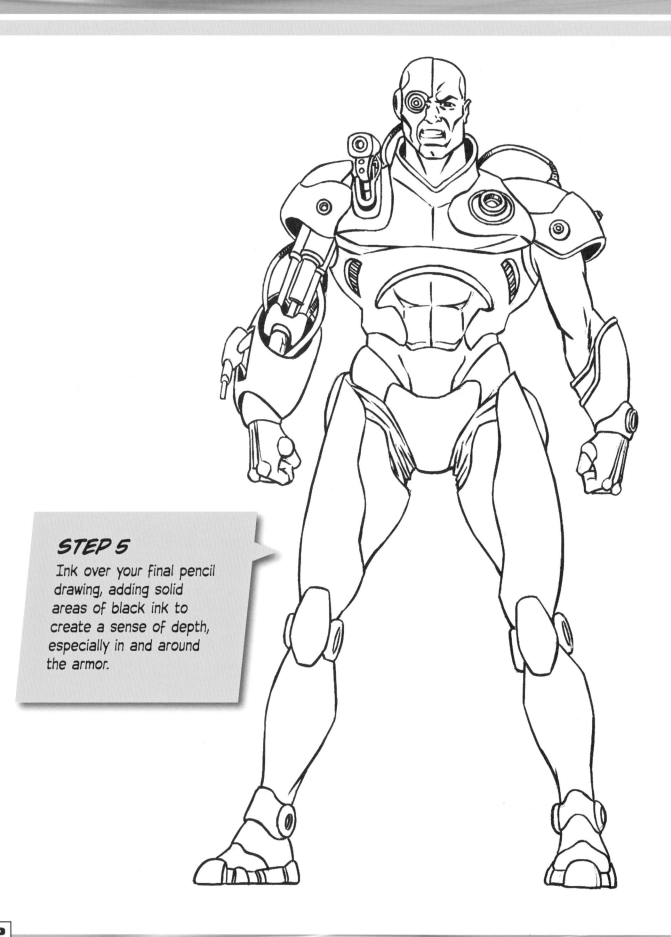

STEP 5

Ink over your final pencil drawing, adding solid areas of black ink to create a sense of depth, especially in and around the armor.

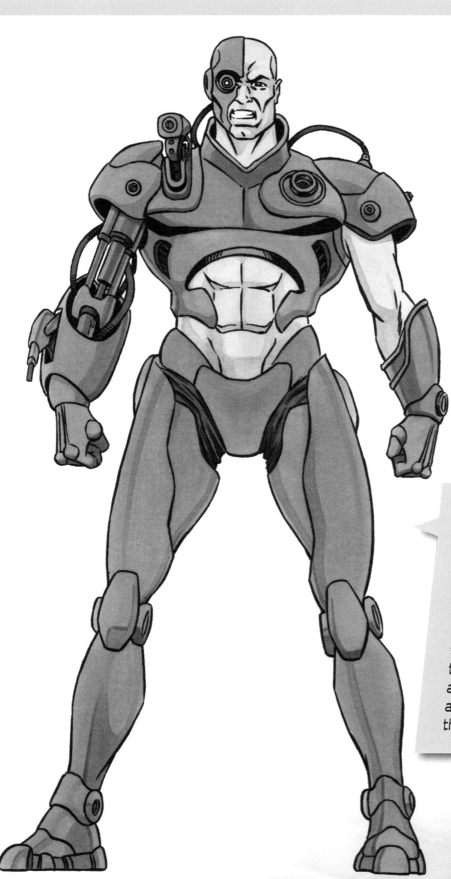

STEP 6

Finally, color your character. The palette for this drawing uses contrasting tones to help distinguish between areas of flesh and those of metal. Warmer tones work for the skin, and cold, metallic blues and grays are best for the armor.

HOW TO DRAW
ALIEN CHARACTERS

SCIENCE FICTION IS AN IMAGINATIVE GENRE. YOU WILL NEED TO BE ABLE TO DRAW CREATURES THAT LOOK VERY DIFFERENT FROM THOSE WE MIGHT FIND ON EARTH. WHAT WILL BE YOUR INSPIRATION?

HUMANOID ALIENS

When you draw a wireframe for a humanoid alien character, consider tweaking and changing the proportions of a normal human. Give them extra limbs, or change the way that their joints work.

SIX EXTRA-LONG ARMS

MULTIPLE EYES LIKE A SPIDER

LEGS WITH TWO KNEE JOINTS

CLOTHING LOOSELY INSPIRED BY THE ANCIENT MIDDLE EAST

As you flesh out the character, think about how the details of their face and body might use features taken from animals here on Earth.

You can find inspiration in clothing from different historical periods or parts of the world. Make sure that your character looks the part for their station in life. This creature is an alien queen.

MONSTROUS ALIENS

When creating an alien monster, it is a good idea to use a combination of Earth creatures as a starting point. This character uses aspects of several creatures, including a woodlouse and a crocodile.

FACE USES ELEMENTS INSPIRED BY CROCODILE AND HIPPO

BODY LIKE WOODLOUSE AND FROG

CUTE CRITTERS

If you want a creature to act like an appealing and lovable companion, you will need to follow certain rules. Large heads, big eyes, and rounded body shapes make for cute creatures. Just about everything else is up to you.

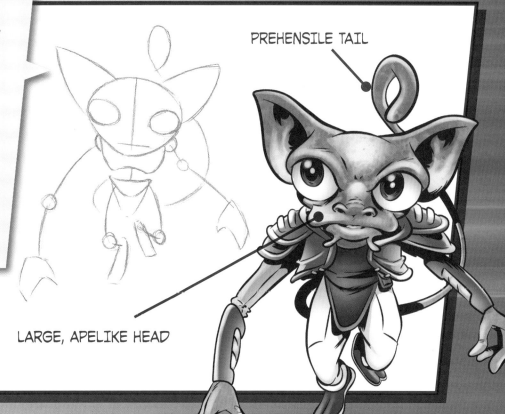

PREHENSILE TAIL

LARGE, APELIKE HEAD

HOW TO DRAW

AN ALIEN BIKER

IT MAY LOOK LIKE SOMEONE HAS STOLEN THIS ALIEN BIKER'S WHEELS, BUT THAT'S NO ORDINARY BIKE HE'S RIDING. IT'S A HOVERBIKE! VRILAK SKREE IS THE LEADER OF A FAMOUS SPACE GANG. NO ONE WOULD BE FOOLISH ENOUGH TO STEAL FROM HIM.

STEP 1

Loosely sketch the circles needed for his head, body, and joints. Give Vrilak elongated arms and legs.

STEP 2

When you're happy with his seated position, add the basic shape of his bike. Play around with different shapes to see what looks best. Build up the outline of his limbs and clothes.

STEP 3

Let your imagination run wild when you fill in the details on his bike and outfit. When creating science fiction vehicles, it's a good idea to look at real, present-day vehicles for inspiration. Use the elements that you think look cool.

STEP 4

Think about where the light is coming from and how it will cast shadows. Lit from above, the underside of the bike will be in darkness, with shaded areas where Vrilak's body blocks the light, too. Keep adding more textural details to his outfit. He loves all kinds of studs, chains, and metal plates!

STEP 5

Take your time at the inking stage. You don't want to ruin your hard work now that you've come this far. You'll need a steady hand for the curves and circles. Keep the lines on the bike to a minimum, so that Vrilak is still the main focus of attention in the image.

STEP 6

You can have fun choosing strange colors for your alien creatures. Vrilak has green skin like a reptile. The silver and red details of his armor stand out nicely against his black jacket and blue pants. His mohican and his shoulder guards match the bodywork of the bike. What a show-off!

HOW TO DRAW
ROBOTS AND STARSHIPS

DRAWING ROBOTS CAN BE DAUNTING. THE IMPORTANT THING TO REMEMBER IS THAT THEY START WITH SIMPLE SHAPES, JUST LIKE DRAWINGS OF PEOPLE. GET THE INITIAL SHAPES RIGHT, AND YOU WILL HAVE A FINISHED ROBOT THAT LOOKS FANTASTIC!

HUMANOID ROBOT

BASIC SHAPES

This demolition droid is made up of flattened disks, tubes, cuboids, and egg shapes.

FINISHED CHARACTER

The fine detail and color transform him! Look out for his heavy-duty blaster arm.

NON-HUMANOID ROBOT

BASIC SHAPES

This medical droid is not based on any familiar human or animal shapes.

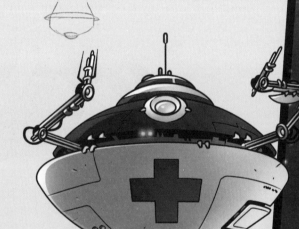

FINISHED CHARACTER

Add as much detail as you like, from lights and antennae to hatches and grasping hands.

SPACESHIPS CAN BE BIG AND BULKY OR SLEEK AND SLIMLINE. YOU CAN COPY THE BASIC SHAPES OF SHIPS FROM OBJECTS YOU FIND AROUND THE HOUSE, SUCH AS HAIR DRYERS OR KITCHEN APPLIANCES.

TRANSPORT SHIP

BASIC SHAPES

This ship is big and bulky, but we have made it narrow at the front.

FINISHED SHIP

The small details on this transport ship, on its tower, for example, give a sense of its size.

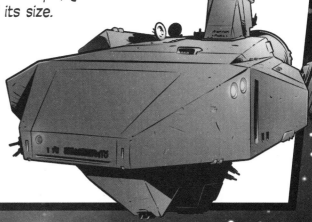

SPACE FIGHTER

BASIC SHAPES

A fighter ship has a pointed nose and several rocket engines behind.

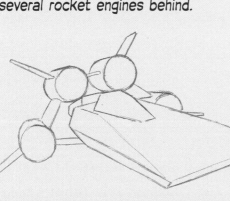

FINISHED SHIP

It needs a hatch on top and battalion colors on the nose tip.

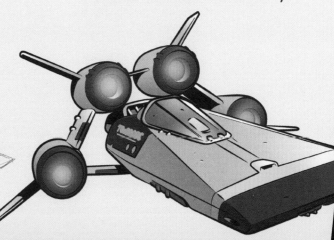

HOW TO DRAW

A GIANT MECHA

NO ONE MESSES WITH A MECHA! CREATE YOUR OWN GIANT ROBOT LIKE GIGANAUT HERE, IN THE BEST TRADITION OF JAPANESE SCIENCE FICTION. CONTROLLED BY A HUMAN PILOT, MECHA ARE BIG ENOUGH TO TACKLE GIANT THREATS, SUCH AS DINOSAUR-LIKE SPACE MONSTERS.

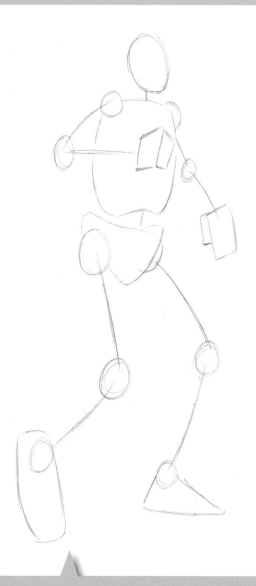

STEP 1
Start with a simple frame. Give your mecha a small head and long legs with huge feet for support.

STEP 2
Build on the frame using basic shapes. Begin to fill out your figure, bulking it up around the shoulders, forearms, and lower legs. Its upper torso should be broad, narrowing at the waist.

STEP 3

Sketch in details such as the fingers and rivets, keeping the mechanical feel of your creation. Add straight lines to show the armor plating on the feet and elsewhere. Keep his helmeted head small in comparison to his body.

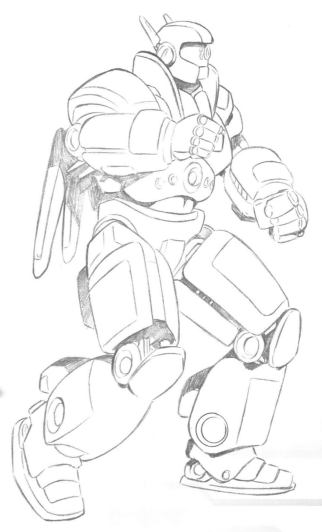

STEP 4

Although he's bulky, Giganaut is agile, and he can run faster than a bullet train. His range of movement is limited by his armor, but the shaded gaps at the knees, waist, elbows, and neck show his flexibility.

STEP 5

Use the inking stage to make your lines crisp and bold. There's nothing fuzzy or unclear about a giant mecha! A fine line pen will allow you to block out the gaps, yet leave in the tiny details in the joints.

STEP 6

A warrior mecha like Giganaut uses bold colors to show off and frighten the opposition. Add glowing green lights with white and pale highlights, and darker shades of red on his armor to show the shadows.

PART 4: FANTASY COMICS

CREATIVE STUDIES

What are the components of a suit of armor? How does an archer hold a bow? Fantasy comic illustrations require a little more background research than artwork for most other types of comics. That's because they involve drawing real, nonimaginary objects, but objects that are not familiar in the present day.

GOLDEN ERA

Most of the artworks in this chapter are based on medieval European history. However, you may wish to research other eras of history for your own story. Why not create a story of doomed love and dragon spirits in ancient China, or a quest for revenge, set among the thunderbirds of Native American mythology?

DRAGON

You might want to create a massive monster for your story. Your hero's source of danger could be a great dragon, an ancient creature that has been summoned to destroy the planet after centuries of slumber.

GOBLINS

Goblins and elves can add moments of humor to a story as well as horror and suspense. Although diminutive in size and easily overpowered in a fair fight, their sly, cunning abilities are often underestimated by the hero.

MUSCULAR MONSTER

Huge, supercharged behemoths that rampage through the story, causing mayhem and destruction, are always welcome in comic books. They guarantee explosive action and good battle scenes for the hero.

WICKED QUEEN

You could give your story a medieval setting and create a kingdom ruled by an evil, powerful king or queen.

HOW TO DRAW

KRALL THE CONQUEROR

IN A FANTASY WORLD OF SORCERORS AND BARBARIANS, YOUR HEROES MAY BE AS WILD AS THE LANDSCAPE. THIS AX-WIELDING WARRIOR IS AS TOUGH AS THEY COME. TAKE CARE WITH YOUR PENCILS, KRALL IS NOT ONE TO MESS WITH!

STEP 1

Establish the warrior's pose by drawing a stick figure, then add basic shapes to this frame. The warrior is strong and muscular, so we need to use bulky construction shapes.

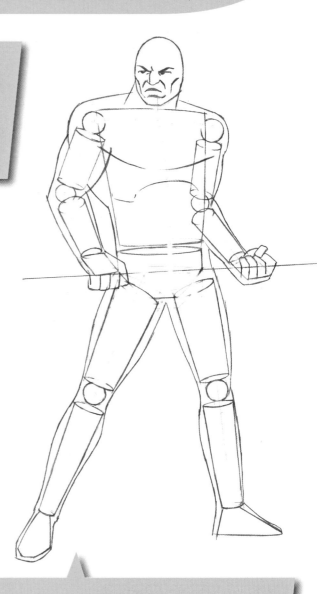

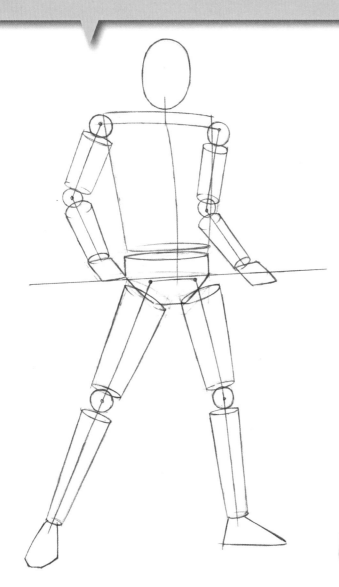

STEP 2

Draw his face and muscles. A strong, square jawline will suit this character. Draw around the construction shapes to create the outline of your figure.

STEP 3

Remove the basic shapes so you're left with a clean outline and begin to add detail. Draw the clothing, in this case an animal fur, a leather belt, and a studded shoulder plate. Draw the warrior's mighty ax.

STEP 4

Clean up the pencil drawing and add any final details. Pencil in areas of light and shade to add depth to your drawing. This will look even more effective once it's inked.

STEP 5
Carefully apply ink over
your pencil drawing.

STEP 6

The final step is to add color. The key to successful coloring is to choose a limited color palette that's not too complex. Here we have used earthy and neutral tones that all work together nicely.

HOW TO DRAW

A MYSTERIOUS ROGUE

"THIS KINGDOM CAN BE A DANGEROUS PLACE," SAYS THE SWORDSMAN, "AND IF YOU'RE SETTING OFF ON A QUEST, THEN YOU'LL NEED A GUIDE." YOUR FIRST CHALLENGE IS TO CAPTURE THE IMAGE OF THIS FRIENDLY STRANGER. HIS NAME IS REX, AND HE'S A DANGEROUS ROGUE!

STEP 1
Sketch a wireframe to show your character's confident stance. Make sure you get his body proportions right.

STEP 2
Loosely pencil in the shape of his limbs, using long, sweeping strokes. Add lines to show the curve of his chest. Draw a cross on his head to show which way it is facing.

STEP 3

Now your imagination can kick in. What is this character thinking? What is he wearing? Where is he going? How does he fit into your story? Our rogue is clothed for the outdoors, with a money pouch on his belt. Is he setting off on a quest?

STEP 4

Firm up your lines, and erase any light sketching you no longer need. Show the folds of the cloak and the creases in his leather boots. Spend some time on his face to get his expression right. You can sense the twinkle in his eye.

STEP 5

At the inking stage, use bold strokes for the outline and smaller, lighter strokes to show texture. Leave sections of his hair unshaded, where the light hits it. The sideways glance, fine lines by his nose and the twitch in his mouth give this rogue a wry, knowing smile.

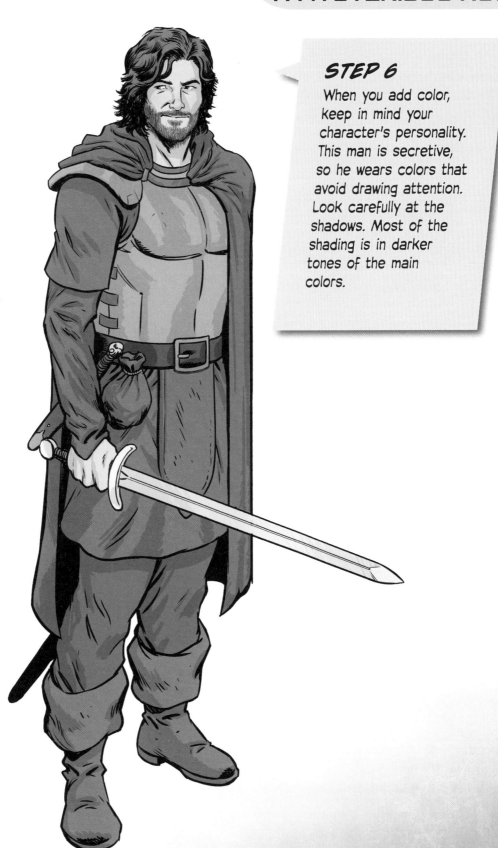

STEP 6

When you add color, keep in mind your character's personality. This man is secretive, so he wears colors that avoid drawing attention. Look carefully at the shadows. Most of the shading is in darker tones of the main colors.

HOW TO DRAW
A WARRIOR QUEEN

WHEN YOU ARE CREATING A FANTASY CHARACTER, THE ONLY LIMIT IS YOUR IMAGINATION. MAJESTRA, THE MALICIOUS MONARCH HAS A DYNAMIC DESIGN THAT COULD BE RECOGNIZED EVEN IN SILHOUETTE.

STEP 1
Build the figure using the stick frame and construction shapes. This warrior queen has a commanding pose.

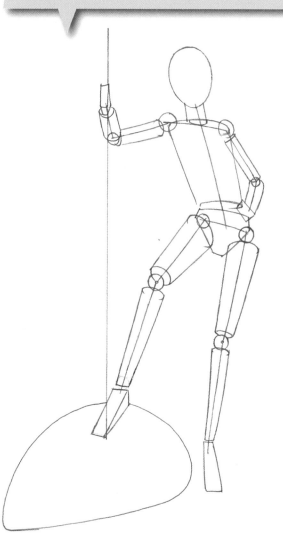

STEP 2
Refine the body shape by outlining around the construction shapes. Give the queen a tough, scornful expression.

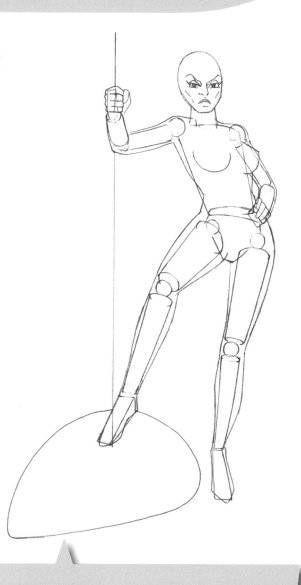

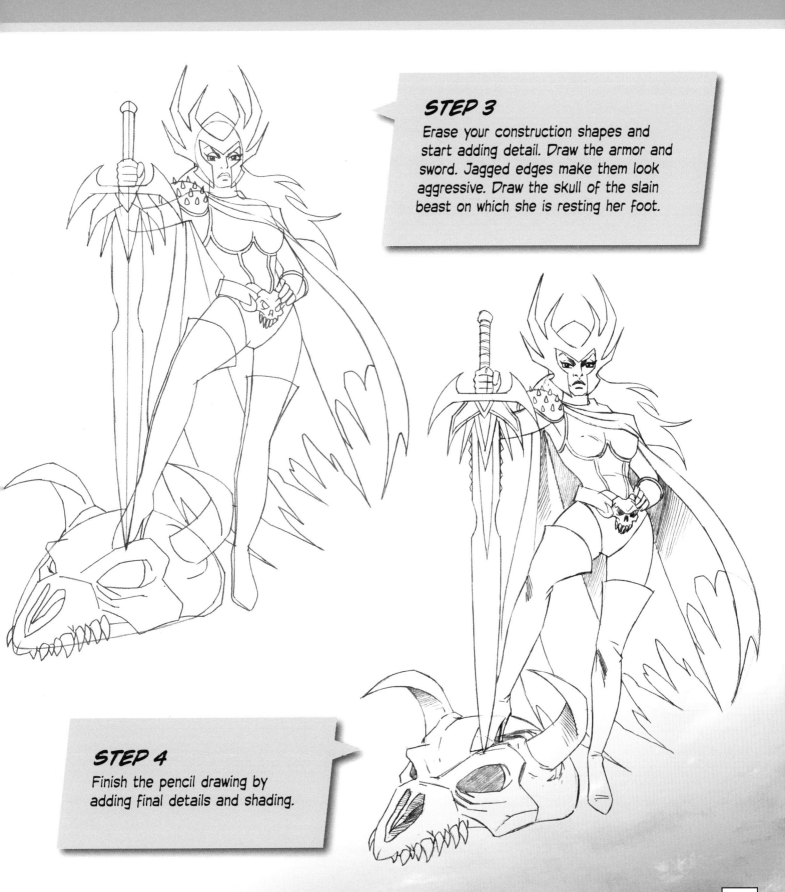

STEP 3

Erase your construction shapes and start adding detail. Draw the armor and sword. Jagged edges make them look aggressive. Draw the skull of the slain beast on which she is resting her foot.

STEP 4

Finish the pencil drawing by adding final details and shading.

STEP 6

Finally, add color to your drawing. For a dramatic effect we have chosen red for the wicked queen's clothing and black for her boots, crown, and hair. Shades of blue are used to create a shiny effect on her hair and boots. Layers of gray are shaded on top of the red base to add depth. Gray and earthy tones are used to color the skull.

WEAPONS AND ARMOR

YOUR FANTASY HEROES WILL NEED TO BE WELL-ARMED! YOU CAN TAKE INSPIRATION FROM DIFFERENT WEAPONS THROUGHOUT HISTORY. YOU HAD BETTER THINK ABOUT SOME PROTECTIVE GEAR, TOO...

BECOME A MASTER SWORDMAKER

You can give your fantasy art a realistic edge by thinking about the details of your characters' equipment. Not all swords are made the same way! What kind of blades and hilts will your characters' swords have?

STRAIGHT SWORDS

A short sword (near left) is made for thrusting, and it may have a guard to protect the hand. A long sword (far left) is swung with both hands, so it needs a long handle.

CURVED SWORDS

Cutlasses (right) have a wide guard and a slightly curved blade for slashing.

MAKE YOUR ARCHERY HIT THE BULLSEYE

When someone is using a bow, their arms are raised high, with the hands in line with each other. The rear elbow is pulled back at a sharp angle, and the head is straight but able to "kiss the string" of the bow. Feet are shoulder-width apart for balance.

The armor worn by your characters speaks volumes about their wealth, status, and fighting ability. It can also say something about their history or backstory: Where have they come from? Is the character a veteran of many campaigns, or have they been thrown into battle against their will?

FULL METAL PLATES

The vulnerable parts of the body are protected with heavy, stiff metal.

MAIL OR CHAIN MAIL

This is made of thousands of tiny metal rings.

LEATHER ARMOR

This very primitive armor is made up of breast panels, cuffs, and a skirt.

READYING YOUR SHIELD

You can really have fun with decorating shields. What will the emblem say about your character or their family? Small shields are used to parry and fight back. Large shields provide the best protection.

BUCKLER

This is a small, round shield, gripped tightly in the fist to deflect the blow of a sword or mace.

HOW TO DRAW

A WOOD-ELF RANGER

THIS FEISTY RANGER MAY NOT BE HEAVILY ARMED, BUT SHE'S NO PUSHOVER. RAVEN SUMMERGLADE IS STRONG AND ATHLETIC, AND SHE'S A MEAN SHOT WITH HER LONGBOW. IT WOULD TAKE A FOOLISH FOE TO TACKLE HER WITH HER DRAGON AT HER SIDE.

STEP 1
Sketch the elf first, standing relaxed with her bow in hand. Then arrange the young dragon's body and wings around her.

STEP 2
Go over your framework, adding the lines of the elf's body and limbs. Flesh out the dragon's tail and head, adding clawed feet and wings held in a folded position.

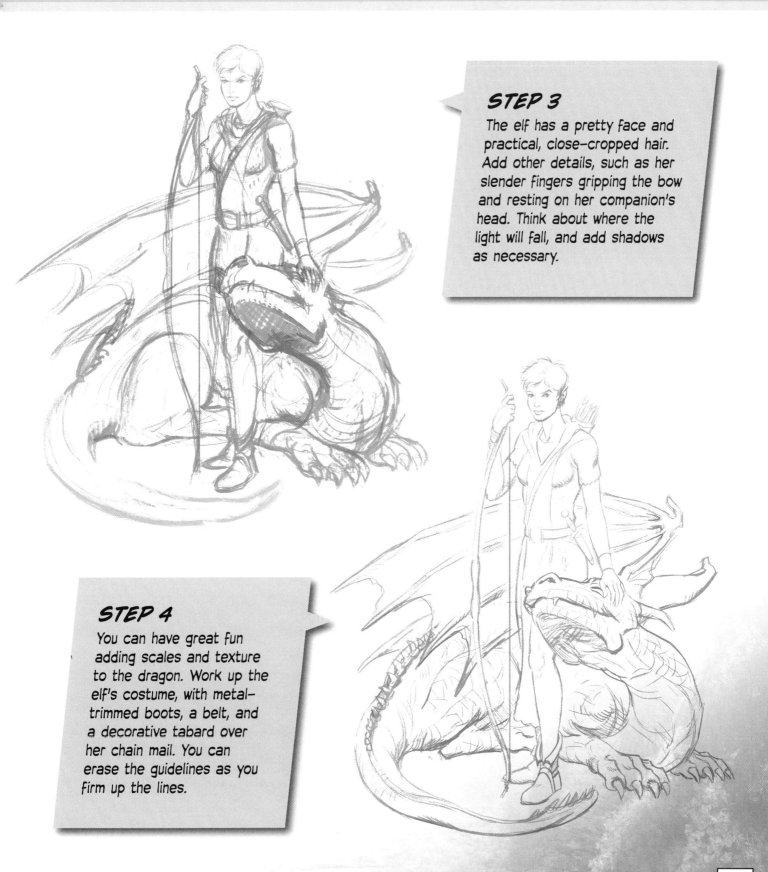

STEP 3

The elf has a pretty face and practical, close-cropped hair. Add other details, such as her slender fingers gripping the bow and resting on her companion's head. Think about where the light will fall, and add shadows as necessary.

STEP 4

You can have great fun adding scales and texture to the dragon. Work up the elf's costume, with metal-trimmed boots, a belt, and a decorative tabard over her chain mail. You can erase the guidelines as you firm up the lines.

STEP 5

Ink over your pencil sketch carefully. Use very fine lines for the elf's facial features. Each claw and spike of the dragon should be precise and neat. Don't rush! There are many small details involved, and you don't want to ruin your hard work.

STEP 6

You don't have to follow normal rules when it comes to coloring fantasy characters. This young ranger has dark skin but silver hair. Match the underside of her dragon's wing to the shades on its belly, with a deeper forest green on top.

IN ANOTHER WORLD...

You can play around with alternative color schemes for your fantasy creations. Where they come from, there are no rules, after all.

HOW TO DRAW
VARIED BUILDS

MANY OF YOUR CREATURES WILL HAVE A NON-HUMAN FORM. YOU
CAN PLAY AROUND WITH PROPORTIONS, CHANGING THE LENGTH
OF LIMBS, SIZE OF THE HEAD AND SO ON, FOR GREAT EFFECTS.

APELIKE CHARACTERS

This swamp troll has long, apelike limbs
and a hunched posture. You can use this
type of build for creatures such as orcs,
goblins, and other primitive beings.

STEP 1

Start with a simple frame. The legs are
bent and unusually long, and the body
is stooped down low to the ground.

STEP 2

Flesh out the body, but not too
much. The creature is thin and
wiry—he looks hungry! Add claws
and webbed feet and hands for a
waterdwelling lifestyle.

SMALL CHARACTERS

Many fantasy stories feature characters with a short and stocky build, such as ancient dwarves that are as tough as nails. For the example here, we are using a halfling thief.

STEP 1

Here, the legs are only two heads high, and the body is just as compact. The feet look large in comparison.

STEP 2

Her body is squat, but as a female, she still narrows at the waist. Her hair and clothes are shorter and wider than normal.

HUGE AND MUSCULAR CHARACTERS

Here is a foul-tempered, brutish mountain troll. You could use this type of heavyset build for big and tough but stupid and slow-moving creatures such as ogres, giants, and Minotaurs.

STEP 1

The troll has a barrel chest and rounded stomach. Notice how long his arms are and what a small head he has.

STEP 2

The lines sketched on his muscles add to the impression of strength and weight. Use plenty of definition on his limbs and body.

HOW TO DRAW

A DWARF WARRIOR

THIS WARRIOR WAS ONCE A MONK, BUT NOW HE'S LIVING THE LIFE OF A PROFESSIONAL MONSTER HUNTER. PATCH IS TINY BUT TOUGH AND WILL TAKE ON ANY OPPONENT, LARGE OR SMALL. THAT'S THE BENEFIT OF CARRYING A LONG—AND MAGICAL—SPEAR.

STEP 1

Use your wireframe to show that the character is ready and alert, with his weight on his front foot, poised for action.

STEP 2

Draw a cross on the head, so that you can position the dwarf's features correctly. Add outlines for his limbs, giving him strong-muscled upper arms and chunky calves and thighs.

STEP 3

Think about your character as you sketch in the important details. Our warrior has lost an eye at some point in his colorful history, so he wears an eyepatch. He has a shaved head but an ornate beard, and the look of a battle-hardened warrior.

STEP 4

Now you can begin to remove some of your rough guidelines. Firm up the details and erase anything unnecessary. Use heavy shading to show the lines of his cloak and his sturdy boots. Finish his beard and face with fine lines.

STEP 5

For the inked version, use solid shading on the underside of his arms, chest, and chin and around the knees. Blacken his eyepatch, and give his good eye a menacing glint. Decorate his buckles and spear to make them his own custom design.

STEP 6

The addition of color draws attention to the details, such as his pierced ear and the dagger tucked into a sheath on his belt. His clothes are shaded in muted colors, but there's no hiding his red beard and eyebrows.

USING PERSPECTIVE
IN FANTASY SCENES

THE USE OF PERSPECTIVE IS AN IMPORTANT SKILL TO MASTER. IT WILL GIVE A FEELING OF DEPTH AND GROUNDING TO YOUR FANTASY SCENES, AND IT IS ESPECIALLY IMPORTANT FOR DRAWING BUILDINGS AND TOWNS.

VANISHING POINT
The straight lines in the scene all meet at a faraway "vanishing point."

PERSPECTIVE LINES
These straight lines show how the buildings should be positioned.

HORIZON
The vanishing point should be placed along an imaginary horizon line.

FORESHORTENING
Things that are closer are drawn larger than things far away. This is known as foreshortening, and it creates the illusion of depth. The buildings along this street become tiny in the distance.

WORM'S-EYE VIEW

Imagine you are viewing a scene from below. The scene has one low vanishing point, across the drawbridge, and another high above the castle, which seems to stretch into the sky.

BIRD'S-EYE VIEW

This picture is drawn as if you are looking at it from high above. It uses two-point perspective, with two vanishing points in different places. Foreshortening makes the tower look smaller than the bird.

HOW TO DRAW

A WIZARDS' BATTLE

NOW YOU CAN PULL TOGETHER EVERYTHING YOU HAVE LEARNED ABOUT CHARACTERIZATION, PROPORTIONS, POSTURE, AND PERSPECTIVE IN ONE DRAMATIC SCENE. THE QUICK-WITTED YOUNG WIZARD, JARYTH, IS SHOWN HERE IN THE MIDST OF A BATTLE AGAINST THE EVIL QUEEN OF ASHES.

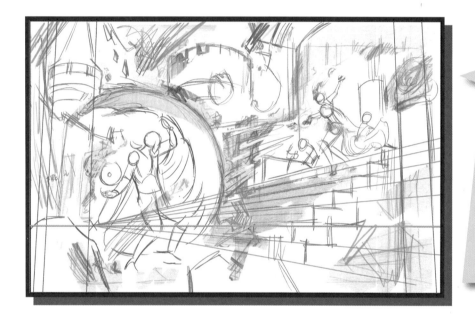

STEP 1

Decide on your vanishing point. Use the lines of the staircase to set up your perspective. Sketch the basic frames for Jaryth and the Queen, her minions, and the background.

STEP 2

Gradually build up the layers of detail in the foreground and background. Now concentrate on your characters. Jaryth is closer to the viewer, so he appears larger than the Queen of Ashes. Add in the details of clothing and the magical "special effects" for the fight.

STEP 3

When you're satisfied with the way the scene is shaping up, you can think more about textures and plan the way that lighting will cast shadows. Add detail to the fiery shield and the pieces falling from the roof.

STEP 4

The inked artwork is dramatic, with strong contrasts of light and dark (this is called "chiaroscuro"). There are no unnecessary lines or shading, but the viewer can spot details like the statues and hooded figures as they take a closer look.

STEP 5

Now you can add dramatic colors to finish your scene. The contrast between the tan backdrop and the red clothes of the Queen of Ashes helps to keep focus on the scarlet-clad villain as well as our heroic wizard.

PART 5: MANGA COMICS

ORIENTAL TWIST

Manga comics can be about the same themes we've already covered—superheroes, science fiction or fantasy. But they also have something that sets them apart as being uniquely Japanese! The manga approach uses many different techniques to European and American comics.

GET THE LOOK

In this chapter you will find tutorials about drawing manga faces and bodies, which use different proportions. There are also dedicated sections covering the Japanese approach to drawing eyes, hair, and facial expressions.

HYPER-ACTION

Manga comics use super-cool, stylized ways of showing motion. Once you have studied the manga approach, you may find that you can adapt elements of it when drawing in a non-Japanese style.

MANGA FIGURES

IT'S IMPORTANT TO THINK ABOUT PROPORTIONS WHEN DRAWING YOUR MANGA CHARACTERS. IF YOUR FIGURES' ARMS OR LEGS ARE THE WRONG LENGTH, THOSE BASIC ERRORS WILL STICK OUT LIKE A SORE THUMB!

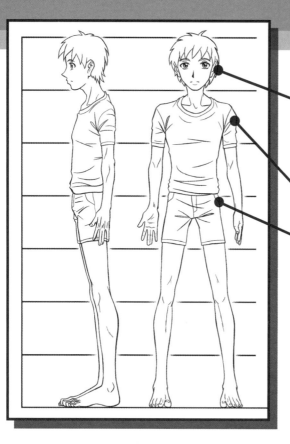

HEADS

Think of your characters' heights in terms of a number of "heads". A typical manga character is about seven heads tall.

SHOULDERS AND HIPS

Male characters are broadest at their shoulders. Female characters are broadest at their hips.

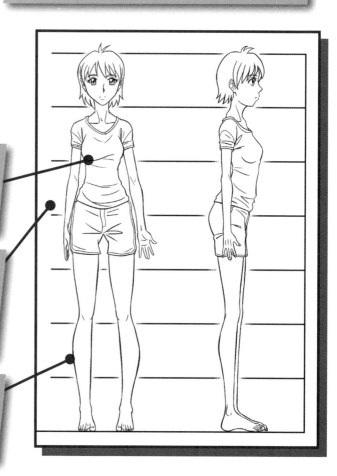

TORSOS

The average character's torso measures about two-and-a-half head lengths.

ARMS

Arms reach from the shoulder down toward the middle of the thigh. Be careful not to give your characters apelike arms!

LEGS

Manga characters' legs measure about four head lengths.

MANGA HEADS

BY REMEMBERING A FEW SIMPLE RULES, YOU CAN MAKE SURE THAT YOUR FACES LOOK APPEALING. THIS WILL ALSO HELP WITH KEEPING FACES CONSISTENT FROM ONE PANEL TO THE NEXT.

FRONT VIEW

In manga, as in real life, eyes are positioned about halfway down the head. But manga eyes are much larger than real ones!

SIDE VIEW

Manga noses are almost invisible when shown head-on. From the side, they are cute and pointed, extending for roughly one eye-height.

BOYS AND GIRLS

Male and female characters both have slim faces. Girls' faces tend to be narrower, with a more pointed chin. They also have longer eyelashes.

EYEBROWS AND EARS

In manga, both male and female eyebrows are narrow and gently arched. Ears extend from the top of the eyes to the bottom of the nose.

HOW TO DRAW

A MONSTER TRAINER

IT'S TIME TO TACKLE YOUR FIRST MANGA CHARACTER! MEET OUR MAGICAL TRAINER, TOKIKO, AND HER TAME MONSTER. THE CREATURE IS A KITSUNE, A MYTHOLOGICAL FOX WITH SUPERNATURAL ABILITIES. KITSUNES HAVE MANY TAILS, WHICH SHOW THEIR AGE AND POWER.

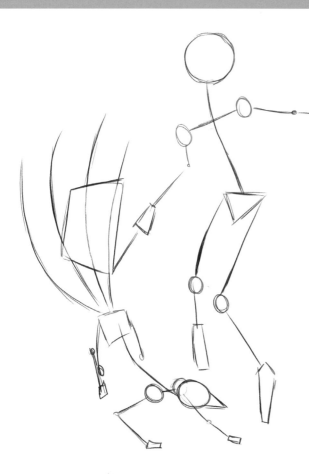

STEP 1
All your sketches should start with a wireframe. This allows you to get the stance and proportions correct.

STEP 2
Roughly sketch in all the elements of the image, from the kitsune's nine tails to the trainer's talismans. She is carrying a magical wand with streamers, called an ounusa.

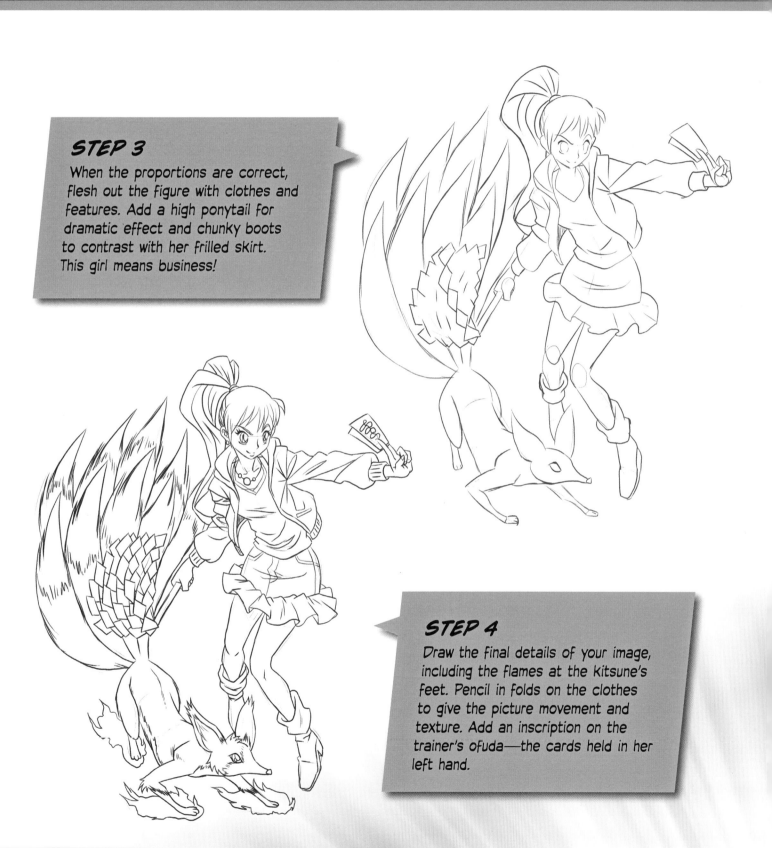

STEP 3

When the proportions are correct, flesh out the figure with clothes and features. Add a high ponytail for dramatic effect and chunky boots to contrast with her frilled skirt. This girl means business!

STEP 4

Draw the final details of your image, including the flames at the kitsune's feet. Pencil in folds on the clothes to give the picture movement and texture. Add an inscription on the trainer's ofuda—the cards held in her left hand.

STEP 5

Trace over the pencil lines of your image with ink. Then use an eraser to clean everything up. A well-inked image should look sharp and crisp. Now you can see the amount of work that goes into every panel of a manga story!

STEP 6

The addition of color is often the most fun part of the process. Manga characters express their personalities through their clothes and hair as well as their faces. Use darker shades of the same colors for shading the image.

MANGA EYES

EYES ARE THE MOST IMPORTANT FEATURES ON A MANGA FACE. THEY ARE USED TO SHOW EMOTIONS AND ALSO HELP TO MAKE CHARACTERS LOOK LIKABLE AND SYMPATHETIC.

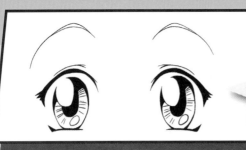

HAPPY EYES

Wide eyes and high eyebrows show happiness. The eyes are very reflective, and the bottom lids curve upward.

SADNESS

Sad characters tend to have actual tears in their eyes. Lower the eyelids and drop the outer eyebrows.

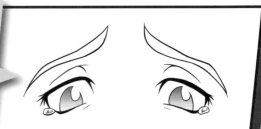

EMBARRASSMENT

The blush lines say "Cringe!" and a sideways glance adds to the impression that this character is feeling shame.

ANGER

The inner eyebrows are dramatically lowered to depict fury. The pupils are small and darker than usual.

FEAR/SHOCK

The contracted pupils have almost disappeared here, but the eyes themselves are large and wide with fear.

MANGA HAIR

HAIRSTYLES CAN SAY A LOT ABOUT A MANGA HERO OR HEROINE. GENERALLY SPEAKING, THE BIGGER THE HAIR, THE WILDER THE CHARACTER!

SPIKY HAIR

Have fun with thick, spiked hair. Frame the face first, and then let it flow backward with jagged tufts.

SMART HAIR

Some manga characters have more realistic hairstyles. If the hair is black, add some white highlights.

RIBBONS

In manga, even tough girls love ribbons! Ponytails are a great device for showing movement.

WINDBLOWN HAIR

It's very common in manga to show hair being blown about by the wind.

HOW TO DRAW

A MARTIAL ARTIST

MOST MANGA FANS LOVE A FIGHT SCENE! CAPTURING A MARTIAL ARTIST IN ACTION CAN BE TRICKY. HOWEVER, IF YOU PAY CAREFUL ATTENTION TO GETTING THE WIREFRAME RIGHT, EVERYTHING ELSE WILL FALL INTO PLACE. OUR FIGHTER, KAZUO, IS WIELDING ENERGY NUNCHAKUS.

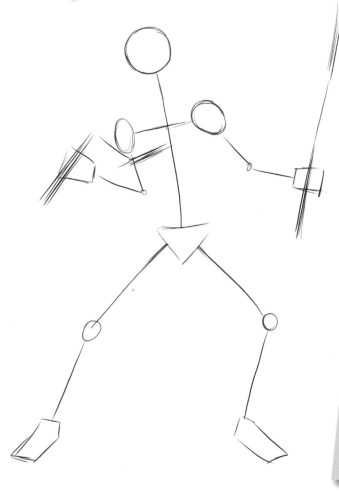

STEP 1
The fighting stance is well-balanced, with legs apart, arms wide, and feet planted securely but ready to spring.

STEP 2
Our fighter may be tough, but like most manga characters, he has a slim build. Take note of how the hands are drawn holding the weapons realistically.

STEP 3

Add more detail to the image. Pay special attention to the movement lines and afterimages left by the whirling weapon. Emphasize the muscles in his arms with small, clean strokes of your pencil.

STEP 4

Kazuo's facial expression tells you he's ready for anything. Even his hair is standing to attention! Sketch in the details of his costume, which features hefty boots, a wide belt, loose combat pants, and a military vest.

STEP 5

Carefully ink over your pencil marks. It's important to get his facial expression right, since that is what the reader's eye will be drawn to. His teeth are gritted, but he is smiling slightly. His arched eyebrows show that he is angry, but perhaps he is relishing the fight.

STEP 6

The basic blue color scheme here is calm, but the flashes of orange add flair and personality. No black is needed for the shading; the folds of his clothes use darker tones of the various blues. Silvery grays show the electric charge of his weapon.

SHOWING EMOTIONS

MANGA HAS ITS OWN WAYS OF SHOWING WHAT PEOPLE ARE FEELING. NOTE THAT THE EMOTIONS ARE CONVEYED BY BOTH THE CHARACTERS' EXPRESSIONS AND BY THE BACKGROUNDS.

ANGRY
Bulging veins in the forehead, often drawn as cross-shaped, are a common way of showing anger.

NERVOUS
His mouth is smiling, but his eyes look worried. A single bead of sweat tells you this guy is flustered or jumpy.

EMBARRASSED
Uh-oh! This isn't a love-flush, this is full-on, shamefaced, megamortified embarrassment. The blush dominates the whole face.

LOVESTRUCK
Flushed cheeks? Wide eyes gazing into the distance? Flowery background? This character is in L.O.V.E.!

CHIBI CARTOONS

IN MANGA, CHARACTERS' EMOTIONS ARE SOMETIMES SHOWN IN AN EXAGGERATED WAY BY DRAWING THE CHARACTERS AS CHIBIS FOR ONE OR MORE PANELS. CHIBIS ARE TINY AND CHILDLIKE, WITH A HEAD THAT'S ALMOST AS LONG AS THEIR BODY.

NERVOUS
The nervous grin is enlarged, and the single bead of sweat is even more exaggerated.

ANGRY
These furious eyes have no pupils. A cross-shaped "anger vein" is floating above her head.

LOVESTRUCK
Just look at those pupils! Love has taken hold, and she's in a dreamworld of her own.

EMBARRASSED
This poor character's blush has deepened, and he's so hot that he's steaming.

HOW TO DRAW

THE DARK RONIN

TAKE A STEP INTO JAPANESE HISTORY WITH THIS TROUBLED WARRIOR. A RONIN IS A MASTERLESS SAMURAI, AND OUR CHARACTER'S STANCE SHOWS HE IS A MASTER OF MARTIAL ARTS AND COMBAT. ALL SAMURAI CARRY TWO SWORDS AND SOMETIMES OTHER WEAPONS, TOO.

STEP 1

Lightly sketch the wireframe, with a guarded stance and two lines for the katanas—long, curved Japanese swords.

STEP 2

Flesh out his broad chest and limbs. This is no skinny samurai! Make sure his hips are narrower than his shoulders. Pay close attention to the position of his legs and feet.

STEP 3

Add to his roguish qualities with long, loose bangs and a wayward ponytail. His samurai uniform covers his chest and thighs, with a sash belt tied at the waist. Both arms should be protected, but it looks like this isn't his first fight...

STEP 4

A lot can be shown about a character by the way you draw his features and also his clothes. This warrior's bandaged wrist speaks volumes, as does his ripped sleeve. Go to town with the detailing on his leather armor.

STEP 5

Up close, you can see the glint in this ronin's eye—the one that isn't obscured by a scar, anyway. Have fun decorating his swords with ornate handle grips. Make sure the bulges of his muscles and the folds of his breeches are fluid and light.

STEP 6

When adding color to the warrior, remember that he is a dark soul with a rebellious streak. The clothing beneath his armor should be drab and plain, but he wears his samurai colors with pride. Keep the colors light on the sharp edges of his swords.

SPEED LINES

MANGA CHARACTERS ARE PART OF A STORYTELLING PROCESS WITH ITS OWN TRICKS AND TECHNIQUES. HERE'S HOW A MANGA ARTIST CARRIES THE READER ALONG WITH THE ACTION WHEN THINGS ARE MOVING FAST!

HORIZONTAL SPEED LINES

Neatly ruled parallel lines show the direction of movement. They can be spaced very tightly to show increased speed but tend to be spaced farther apart around elements like the face.

RADIAL SPEED LINES

A starburst of lines spreading from a central point can show rapid movement toward or away from the reader. The blank space where the lines would meet is the far distance.

SPECIAL EFFECTS

PATTERNED MANGA BACKGROUNDS DO THREE THINGS: THEY GRAB THE READER'S ATTENTION, THEY SHOW CHARACTERS' REACTIONS WITHOUT WORDS, AND THEY MAKE FOR AN INTERESTING BREAK FROM STANDARD BACKGROUND SCENERY.

SURPRISE!

What's happening here? The startling background grabs your attention and makes you want to know more. It's something amazing, judging by the lightning flashes!

FOCUS LINES

An explosion of lines drawn outward from a focal point makes you instantly aware of what's important in a scene. This can add to the feeling of drama and excitement.

HOW TO DRAW
A DOJO SCENE

YOU'VE PRACTICED DRAWING CHARACTERS WITH VARIED EXPRESSIONS AND MOVEMENTS, AND ADDING DRAMATIC EFFECTS. NOW IT'S TIME TO PUT ALL THOSE SKILLS TOGETHER TO CREATE AN ACTION-PACKED SCENE IN WHICH SEVERAL CHARACTERS INTERACT WITH EACH OTHER.

STEP 1

Take some time to sketch the position of each character. They should feel like they are interacting in a dramatic way. Where are they each looking? What are they about to do?

STEP 2

When you are happy with how the characters fill the frame, sketch in the basic lines of the background. Flesh out each of the characters, making sure they are all in proportion to each other.

STEP 3

Slowly build up the details of the characters and scenery. Don't ruin your hard work by rushing! Ask yourself: do any areas of the image need more interest? We added some empty robes at the bottom left, to suggest that the ninjas can turn to smoke.

STEP 4

As you ink the image, make sure that it's clear what's happening. Who are the good guys and who are the bad guys? Your scene is telling a story, so it's up to you to show what's taking place. Never lose sight of the big picture!

FEARLESS FACES

Remember what you have learned about manga features. Give your heroes big eyes and expressions of brave determination to contrast them with the masked baddies.

STEP 5
Finally, use your coloring to highlight the main characters and make the villains look sinister. Use bold shades in the center, and play with the special effects, adding flames, sparks, and force fields.

GOING FOR GOLD
Bring the decoration to life with white-gold highlights and brown-gold shading.

GLOWING EYES
Leave the middle of the ninjas' eyes bright white, but color the area around them red.

PART 6: HORROR COMICS

We've previously covered various different aspects of drawing backgrounds and scenes. But what is a scene without an atmosphere? In this section, you'll discover how to use inking to create mysterious and sinister moods.

You already know how to use color to express character and reveal light sources. With horror comics, the light and dark are more extreme, drawing attention to fearful faces while hiding danger in the shadows.

You can use these skills to create a masterpiece of horror storytelling... or apply the same rules to add atmosphere to any type of comic story!

HOW ATMOSPHERIC!

A SCENE CAN BE COMPLETELY TRANSFORMED BY THE EFFECTIVE USE OF SHADOWS. A SETTING THAT WOULD APPEAR ORDINARY OR EVEN WELCOMING IN GOOD LIGHTING CAN SUDDENLY BECOME MYSTERIOUS AND SINISTER.

A SCENE WITHOUT SHADOWS

This library scene could be any ordinary library, although the costumes give a visual clue that it is a historical setting. The light source is unclear: is light streaming through the stained-glass window or coming from the ceiling lamp?

A SCENE WITH SHADOWS

The artist has added some shadows to this inked version of the image. It feels much more atmospheric, though it is not necessarily a horror scene. The shadows are cast by the books, people, and furniture as the light shines in through the large window on the left.

A SCENE WITH HEAVY SHADOWS

Now it's clearer that our scene is spine-chilling and spooky! Much of the room is inked out in shadow, allowing us to focus on the characters in the foreground. Remember, the bold contrast between light and dark is called chiaroscuro.

HOW TO DRAW

A SWAMP ZOMBIE

THIS CREEPY CREATURE HAS BEEN LYING IN WAIT BENEATH THE FOUL, STAGNANT WATERS OF AN ANCIENT SWAMP. NOW IT HAS FINALLY EMERGED, AND IT LOOKS LIKES IT'S HUNGRY FOR HUMAN FLESH! CAN YOU CAPTURE ITS FRIGHTENING POSE AND EXPRESSION?

STEP 1

Use a wireframe to plan how you want your creature to stand and how long its limbs will be. It's tall and skinny.

STEP 2

Develop the hands and feet with fingers and toes. Use curved lines to outline the thin legs and arms. Connect the hips and chest with a narrow waist, and sketch in facial features.

STEP 3

Add more details. Work up the hollow face with its gaping mouth. Add holes for the eyes and nose. Begin to sketch the loose rags hanging from its body. Use scratchy lines to create ragged edges.

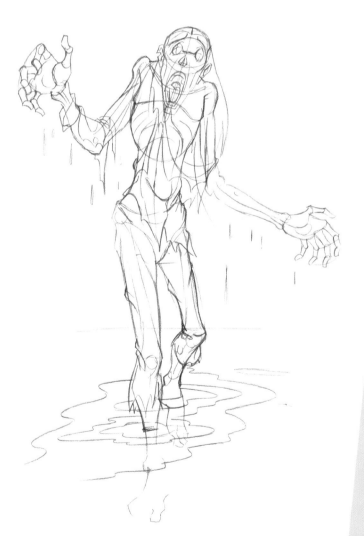

STEP 4

Erase any guidelines you no longer need, and finish off the details of the creature's clothes, face, and hair. Its ribs are clearly visible underneath its cold, damp flesh. Add small details, such as buttons on its shirt and holes in its pants.

STEP 5

Now carefully trace your pencil lines in ink. Use different thicknesses of stroke: thinner ones for details and thicker ones for the outline. Draw some blotches on the skin. Add dark patches where shadows fall on its clothing, mouth, nose, hair, and ribs.

STEP 6

You can use color to suggest texture and temperature in a picture like this. The green and blue colors we have chosen make this swamp zombie look deathly cold. The yellow sheen on its flesh and clothes makes it look slimy and damp.

HOW TO DRAW
A HAUNTED SCARECROW

THIS PUMPKIN-HEADED SCARECROW HAS BEEN BROUGHT TO LIFE BY
A SPIRIT OF VENGEANCE FROM BEYOND THE GRAVE. BEWARE OF ITS
CLAWLIKE HANDS AND SHARP-PRONGED PITCHFORK! WHAT KIND OF
SPOOKY STORIES WILL IT INSPIRE YOU TO ILLUSTRATE?

STEP 1
Body language plays an important
role in making a creature look
sinister. Is this scarecrow warning
us away from something?

STEP 2
Bulk out its frame, giving definition to
its skinny arms and legs. Take time to
sketch each joint and knuckle for its
outstretched, clawlike hand.

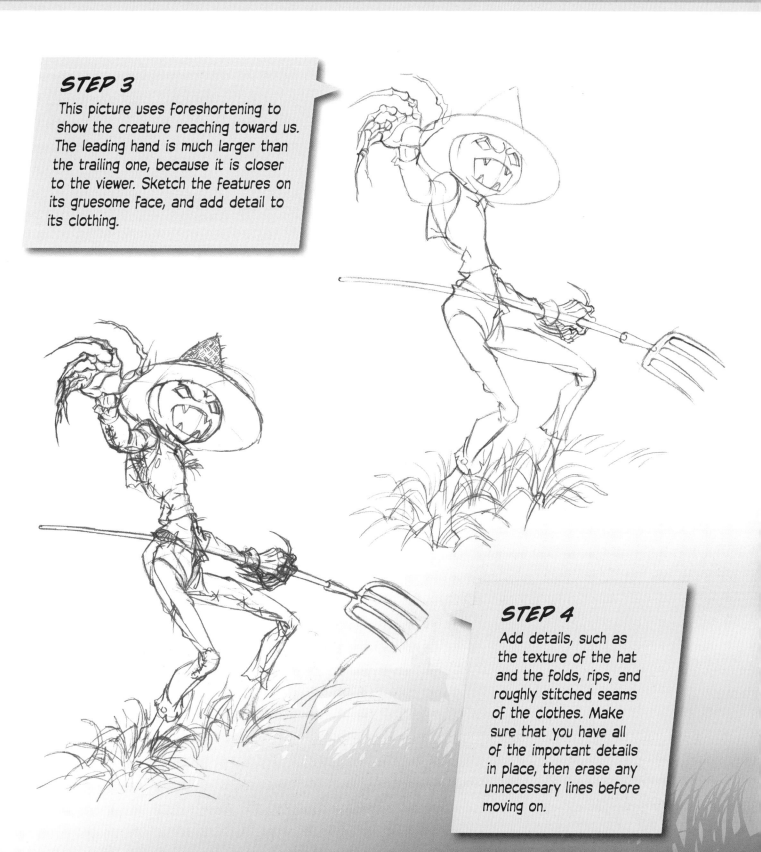

STEP 3

This picture uses foreshortening to show the creature reaching toward us. The leading hand is much larger than the trailing one, because it is closer to the viewer. Sketch the features on its gruesome face, and add detail to its clothing.

STEP 4

Add details, such as the texture of the hat and the folds, rips, and roughly stitched seams of the clothes. Make sure that you have all of the important details in place, then erase any unnecessary lines before moving on.

STEP 5

Ink your scarecrow carefully
with a black pen. You will
need to use very fine lines
for the textural details, such
as the straw poking through
its clothing. Use a slightly
broader pen for its outline.
Then fill in the shadows on
its shins and feet and the
black grass.

STEP 6

We have added more shadows at the coloring stage. Use dark blocks of color for the body and grabbing hand, with pale highlights on the left edge of each shape to give it definition. The pumpkin head is glowing from within, so the brightest orange appears in the mouth and eyes.

PART 7: ADVANCED SKILLS

SPLASH PAGE

Comic books sometimes begin with a splash page, which draws the reader into the story. They can also be used to give extra punch to the most dramatic moments in a story, such as when the mysterious villain reveals his true identity or the hero falls from a cliff edge.

A splash page has to be attention grabbing. In this example, heavy shadow and an unusual point of view have been used to create atmosphere.

Narrative captions can be used to tell the story or to reveal a character's thoughts. However, you should never give the same information in the picture and text.

DEX LARROCA WAS RUNNING OUT OF TIME. IF HE WAS TO BUST THIS CASE WIDE OPEN, HE'D HAVE TO RESORT TO THE TOUGHEST KIND OF CRIME INVESTIGATION—THE HARD-BOILED KIND!

STANDARD PAGE

This is the most common type of comic page.

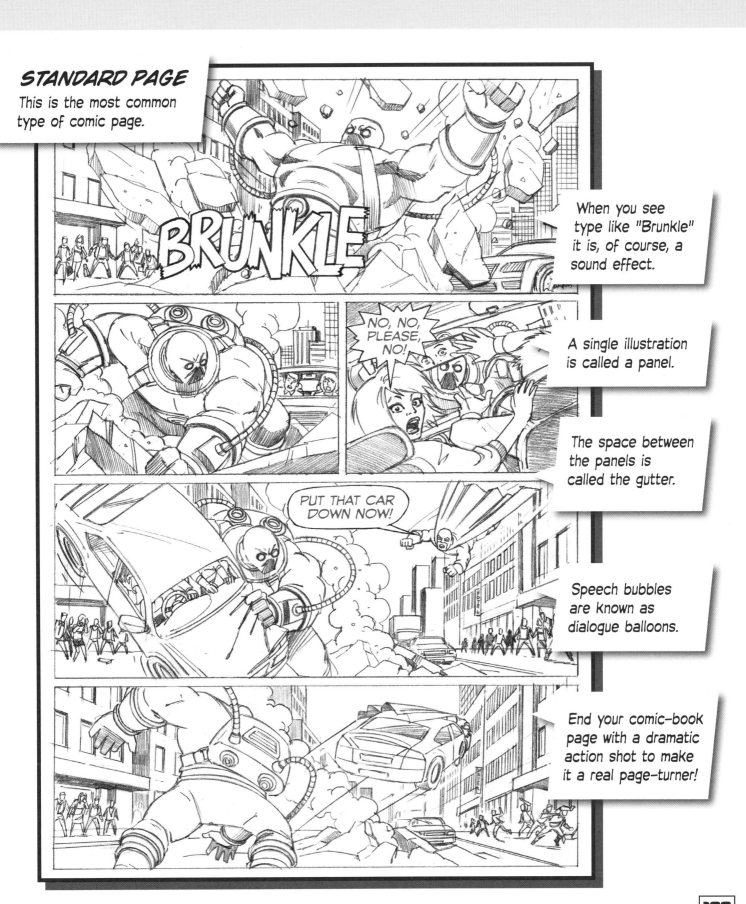

When you see type like "Brunkle" it is, of course, a sound effect.

A single illustration is called a panel.

The space between the panels is called the gutter.

Speech bubbles are known as dialogue balloons.

End your comic-book page with a dramatic action shot to make it a real page-turner!

COMPOSITION

TYPES OF PANELS

PLANNING A COMIC BOOK IS SIMILAR TO MAKING A FILM. A FILM DIRECTOR CHOOSES THE POSITION FROM WHICH THE CAMERA WILL GET THE MOST EFFECTIVE SHOT. AS THE ARTIST, IT'S UP TO YOU TO FIND ANGLES THAT WILL ILLUSTRATE THE PLOT CLEARLY, WHILE KEEPING THE READER INTERESTED.

This panel is called a close-up. This is where you zoom in very closely on the action. Close-ups are often used to focus on a character's facial expressions and emotions.

The panel below is called a medium shot. The action is viewed from nearby, and the reader can see the figures from head to toe.

This panel is called a long shot or panoramic shot. It is used when the story requires a wide-angle view to show the setting, rather than focusing on the characters.

Here is another long shot, but this time the action is seen from above, as a bird's-eye view.

This angle is called a worm's-eye view. It shows the action from below.

Here, the main details are shown in solid black. This is called a silhouette.

COMPOSITION
STORYTELLING

YOUR CHOICE OF PANEL TYPE AFFECTS THE STORY. COMPOSITION, OR LAYOUT, AND IS A VERY IMPORTANT PART OF COMIC BOOK CREATING. EACH PANEL MUST BE CAREFULLY COMPOSED SO THAT THE STORY IS EASY TO FOLLOW. THE ACTION SHOULD FLOW FROM PANEL TO PANEL IN A WAY THAT IS EYE-CATCHING.

SETTING THE SCENE

This long shot has been chosen to set up the story. It leaves the reader eager to discover what will happen next.

Readers in the West normally scan a page from left to right and top to bottom. Notice how the elements in this panel flow from left to right. This is the order in which they will be viewed.

PACKING IN INFORMATION

This wide-angle shot is bursting with action and information. All the elements work logically so that the reader can immediately understand the story. A comic-book page should be drawn so that it all makes sense without the aid of captions or dialogue balloons.

FRAMING THE ACTION

Here is a close-up shot. It's an intense scene in which the hero is rushing to save a woman who is trapped in a burning building. Notice how the main interest is grouped in the top half of the frame. The smoke, below, is used to frame the action.

DRAMATIC SHAPES

Here is another wide shot. Notice how the position of the woman's body forms a triangle. The forest makes a curve around her.

HOW TO DRAW

A HORROR STORY

COMIC ART IS ABOUT MORE THAN JUST INDIVIDUAL IMAGES! A REAL COMIC ARTIST TELLS A DYNAMIC STORY THROUGH A SEQUENCE OF PANELS. IN THIS PROJECT, YOU CAN PUT TOGETHER ALL THE SKILLS YOU'VE LEARNED IN THIS BOOK TO CREATE A FINISHED COMICS PAGE.

STEP 1
Decide what your story is and how many frames you need to tell it. Then create a rough sketch of the page. Don't try to fit too much into each frame. In our first panel, the scene is set with a mystery character at the foot of a creepy staircase. In the second and third panels, they approach a door and open it to reveal what's inside. Then the main action happens in the final panel, when the character is revealed as a monster!

STEP 2

Take a careful look at your rough page. Do you want to make any changes before you add details to the pencil sketches? We decided to flip the first panel around, so that the reader's eye falls on the shadow on the staircase before anything else. This creates a nice sense of tension. Notice the way that the jumping character in the final panel overlaps with the top edge of the panel. It's an excellent way of giving a panel extra excitement.

STEP 3

We've really gone to town with the shadows at the inking stage. By using plenty of black, you can show readers that this is a chilling tale and put them on edge. Notice that we have not lost any detail, though, because we have used narrow white lines to show shapes and textures within the shadowy areas.

STEP 4

The color version of this story cleverly uses light and shade, too. Your eye seeks the detail in the top scene, and then it is drawn to the light farther down. Clever details, such as the yellow keyhole in frame two, link the panels together and give visual clues to what is happening and where the action is taking place.

HOW TO DRAW

A SUPERHERO STORY

THE PLOT—A HUGE MONSTER IS RAMPAGING THROUGH THE CENTER OF A BIG CITY. THE CREATURE LIFTS A CAR, TERRIFYING ITS PASSENGERS. JUST AT THIS MOMENT, OUR HERO, OMEGAMAN, ARRIVES AT THE SCENE AND THE MONSTER ATTACKS!

STEP 1: FIRST DRAFT

A first draft is all about figuring out how the action will flow from panel to panel. The figures are drawn very roughly, first in stick figure form then with simple construction shapes.

PERSPECTIVE

Draw perspective lines so you get the angle of the buildings right, and sketch a rough grid to help you scale the foreground and background objects correctly in relation to one another.

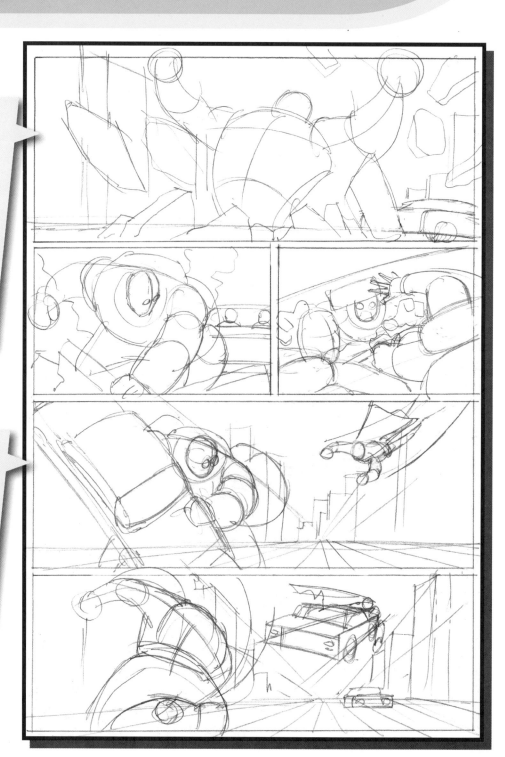

STEP 2: ADDING DETAIL

Start to flesh out your figures and add detail. This page is packed with action, so keep your figures looking dynamic.

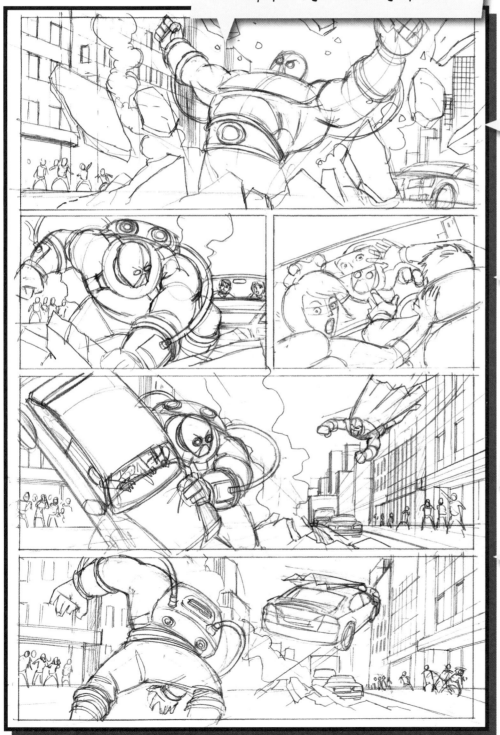

BUILDINGS

Using the perspective lines that you drew at the first draft stage, map out the shapes of the buildings and their various heights. Take care to draw the windows of each building accurately.

CARS

Base the cars on real vehicles. You could look at some parked cars in your street or neighborhood and do some sketches. If you base your content on real objects and pay attention to detail, your drawings will look much more realistic and polished.

DON'T RUSH!

The more time you spend getting all the little details right at this stage, the more believable your final page will look.

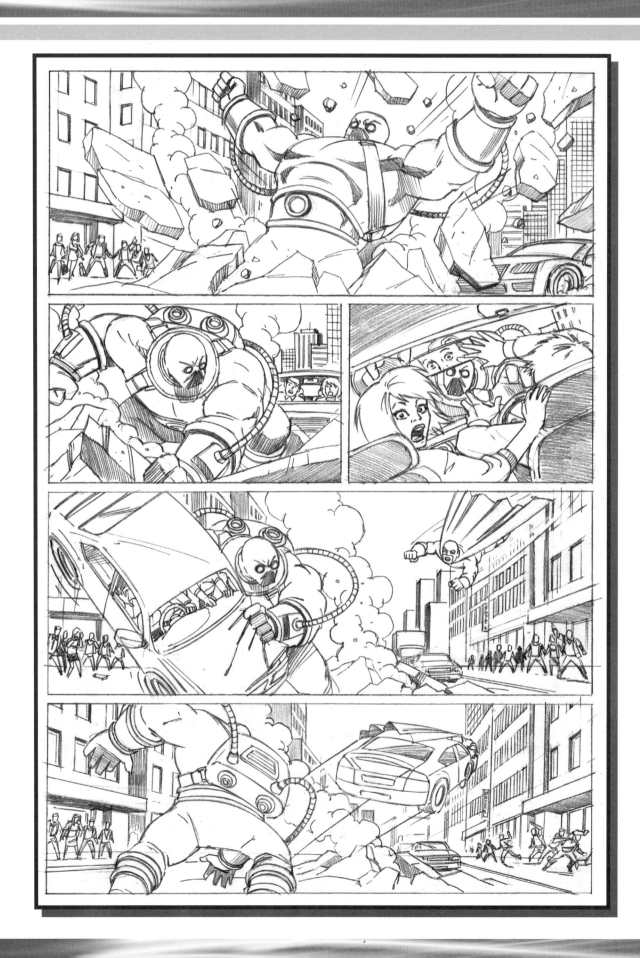

STEP 3: THE FINAL PENCILED PAGE

Look at the finished page opposite. As you can see, we haven't included any text in this pencil page. This is to demonstrate how, when drawn correctly, a series of panels can clearly tell a story without any dialogue. The guide below gives a description of each panel.

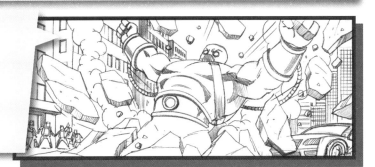

PANEL 1

This shows the entrance of the crazy monster as it smashes up through the road, scattering debris everywhere. We also see a car screeching to a halt on the far right. This is the reader's first sight of the monster's victims.

PANEL 3

We now switch to a point of view inside the car, as the monster approaches and grabs the hood.

PANEL 2

Next, the monster climbs out of the hole in the ground and notices the car and its passengers.

PANEL 4

A wide shot shows both the monster and the hero rushing to the rescue. The monster turns its back away from the hero, holding the car like a weapon...

PANEL 5

The monster hurls the car with the passengers still inside at Omegaman. But what happens next?

STEP 4: INKING

Take time to carefully ink over the pencil drawing.

INKING TOOLS

A technical inking pen has been used for the straight lines. A brush ink pen has been used for the linework in the foreground.

TYPES OF LINES

Different line widths can make objects look distant or close. Use light, thin linework for objects in the background. Use bolder linework for the objects in the foreground so that they stand out. This will make the drawing look less flat.

STEP 5: COLORING

This scene is set in the daytime, so a pale blue sky has been used in all panels. The buildings are a mixture of off-white, sand, beige, and pale grays. A cool gray has been used for the road and scarlet for the car.

HEROIC HUES

The colors we have chosen for the superhero are sky blue for the mask and cape and pale blue for the body.

SINISTER SHADES

The villain's costume has been colored using a light blue overlayed with gray. The metallic parts of the suit have been colored cadmium yellow. A cool gray has been chosen for the boots.

HOW TO DRAW
A CRIME STORY

THE PLOT—HARD-BOILED COP DEX LARROCA IS HOPING TO ARREST A DANGEROUS CRIMINAL. HE FOLLOWS A LEAD TO AN ABANDONED WAREHOUSE AND BREAKS IN TO SEARCH THE BUILDING.

STEP 1: FIRST DRAFT

Rough out the story in the panels using simple shapes to establish the composition and content of each one.

Consider the different types of panels and which angle will work best for each step of the action. Remember to keep it simple but exciting!

Stop every so often and take a look at the whole page. Ensure the story makes sense from panel to panel before you add any detail.

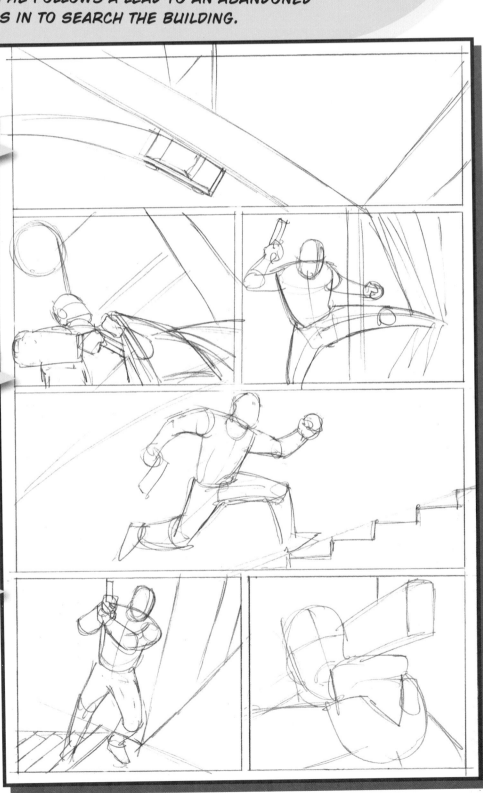

STEP 2: ADDING DETAIL

Once you are happy that the series of panels works effectively, start to add more detail to your layout.

ON THE GRID

Use grid lines to help get the perspective correct. As there needs to be lots of different viewpoints and angles from panel to panel, you need to be careful to get the perspective just right on each one. Grids are also useful for accurately plotting where the windows of buildings should go.

CONSISTENCY

Try to keep the look of your character consistent from panel to panel. Do lots of sketches before you start to draw a whole page, so you know every detail of your character's appearance.

STEP 3: THE FINAL PENCILED PAGE

On the page opposite you can see Dex Larroca in action in the finished comic-book page. See how shading and fine details have been added, such as the timberwork on the boarded-up windows and exposed brickwork where plaster has broken away. The final panel of the story leaves the reader guessing who or what might be waiting for Dex as he turns the corner.

PANEL 1

We open with a bird's-eye view of Dex pulling up outside the warehouse. This angle is excellent for establishing a location. It also makes the reader feel that the character is being watched.

PANEL 2

Here we have a worm's-eye view as Dex gets ready to enter the building.

PANEL 3

This is a straight-on medium shot.

PANEL 4

This is a kind of wide-angle medium shot. It gives a strong sense of sideways movement.

PANEL 5

Again, this angle suggests that Dex may be being secretly observed by someone outside the panel. This creates extra suspense and a feeling of unease in the reader.

PANEL 6

Finally, we cut to an intense close-up as Dex turns the corner. He shouts, "FREEZE!"

STEP 4: INKING

Trace over your pencil lines, again using stronger, thicker lines for the objects in the foreground.

CRIME NOIR

Notice how some areas are filled with solid black. For example, the sides of buildings, the stairs and Dex's legs and feet are filled with ink. This is not strictly realistic, but it gives a nice sense of weight and contrast to your artwork. Heavy use of solid ink blocks is especially popular in crime and horror comics.

FREEZE!

STEP 5: COLORING

A different color palette is used in the first three and second three panels. This gives a different feeling to the outdoor and indoor scenes.

OUTDOOR COLORS

A base color of pale blue was applied to panels 1, 2, and 3 so that when other colors were added over the top it would give a moonlit tone to the scene.

INDOOR COLORS

Panels 4, 5, and 6 are inside the building. Dark tones of gray were used to give the place a gritty, poorly lit feel. A very pale gray was also used as a base for the detective.

HOW TO DRAW
A SCI-FI STORY

SPACE PILOTS ZAK AND LARA RETURN TO THEIR SATELLITE HEADQUARTERS TO FIND THAT IT HAS BEEN INFESTED BY ALIENS. AND NOT JUST ANY ALIENS, BUT THE MOST DANGEROUS KIND OF ALL: MAN-EATING SPACE APES!

STEP 1: FIRST LAYOUT

It's a good idea to experiment with different layouts. Your page must be dynamic and exciting but also easy to read.

WHAT'S WRONG HERE?

The panels in this layout are all roughly the same size, which gives us very little space for the action. The characters are more or less viewed from the same angle and distance throughout. The layout could be much more dynamic and varied, and the final panel would work better with more room to breathe.

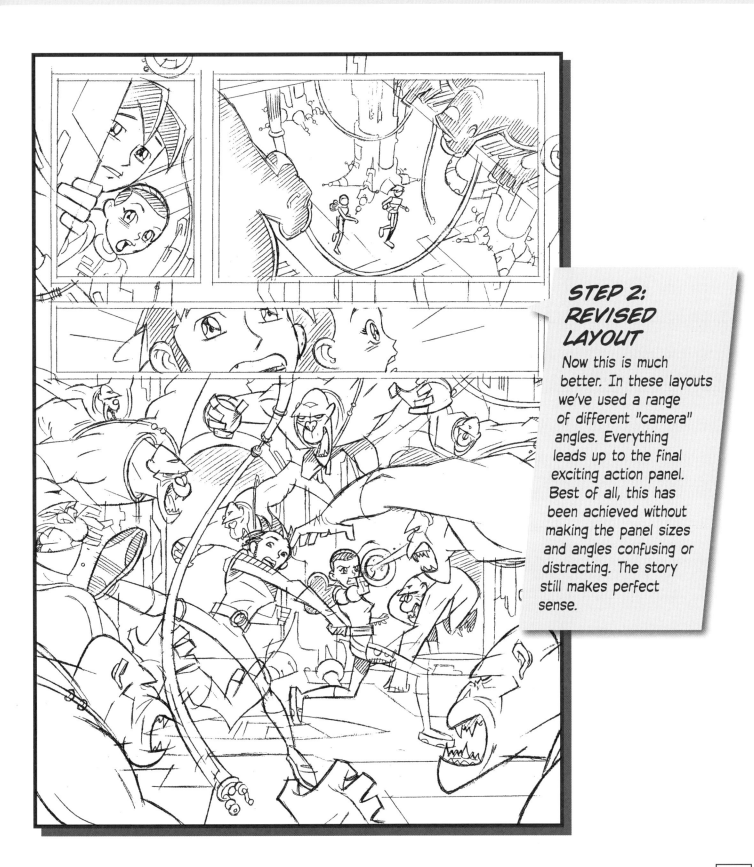

STEP 2: REVISED LAYOUT

Now this is much better. In these layouts we've used a range of different "camera" angles. Everything leads up to the final exciting action panel. Best of all, this has been achieved without making the panel sizes and angles confusing or distracting. The story still makes perfect sense.

STEP 3: INKING

This page has been inked with sharp, neat lines. Heavier lines are used for the outlines of objects.

The edges of the panels have been given a very thick, stylized line. Notice how the gutters of the first three images are part of the large image below.

STEP 4: COLORING

Here's the finished page. The main palette that we have chosen for this page is a mixture of purple and gray. Zak and Lara stand out against this background because of their contrasting red and blue costume colors.

COMPUTER COLORS

Unlike the previous colored pages, which were colored in a traditional way, this page has been colored using a computer. The inked artwork was scanned into the computer, and the program Photoshop was used for coloring.

COMPOSITION

"CAMERA ANGLES"

THERE ARE MANY DIFFERENT WAYS TO TELL A COMIC STORY. AN ARTIST MUST CHOOSE THE BEST ANGLES AND DISTANCES FOR EACH PANEL. IN THIS SHORT SPOOKY STORY, WE SHOW AN EXPLORER OPENING A MYSTERIOUS STONE DOOR, ONLY TO BE GREETED BY A WEREWOLF!

FIRST ATTEMPT

This version of the scene isn't terrible, but it's rather static and boring. The panels are all the same size. The characters are shown from a similar distance, and the viewpoints chosen do not do enough to create a sense of urgency or drama. The reader understands the story but is not drawn in.

SECOND ATTEMPT

This second version of the scene is much more exciting. The panel shapes are interesting, and close-up shots are mixed with longer shots and varied angles. However, there is so much going on that the scene has become confused. And what is happening in the last panel? Is it even in the same place?

THIRD ATTEMPT

This third version of the scene gets the balance just right. The storytelling is nice and clear—it's not hard for the reader to tell what has happened. However, there is plenty of variation in the distance and angle from which we see the action, and there is a well-planned sense of drama and excitement.

COVER DESIGN

THE HEROIC POSE

THE MOST IMPORTANT PART OF A COMIC OR GRAPHIC NOVEL IS ITS COVER.
THE DESIGN AND ARTWORK MUST GRAB THE INTEREST OF A POTENTIAL READER.
WE'LL LOOK AT SEVERAL DIFFERENT APPROACHES TO A FRONT COVER.
THE FIRST SHOWS AN ICONIC HERO IN A DYNAMIC POSE.

STEP 1: ROUGHS

The first stage of the design process is the creation of thumbnail roughs. These are small, simple sketches and layouts of potential cover designs.

FIRST ROUGH

In this example, the hero, Omegaman, is standing on a rooftop, surveying the city. We can immediately tell he is strong, brave, and ready for action. This type of cover design is often used for first issue covers.

SECOND ROUGH

This second attempt at a cover design shows our lead character looking nobly into the distance, with the moon looming behind him. The gargoyle has been dropped from the bottom of the image.

STEP 2: PENCILS

Now we need to choose the most effective elements from each rough to use on the final cover. We've chosen to keep the gargoyle from the first rough. We've taken the upright pose from the second rough, as well as the use of the moon as a framing device.

STEP 3: INKS

Once the cover design has been finalized and drawn in pencil, black ink can be applied. Always remember to leave enough space in your artwork for the cover type—this is the title of your comic book and any other information you wish to include. The sky on this cover could have been inked in solid black, which would also have been dramatic. However, this would have left very little room for color. Use bold line work to make your drawing punchy and powerful. Remember, this cover has to grab attention!

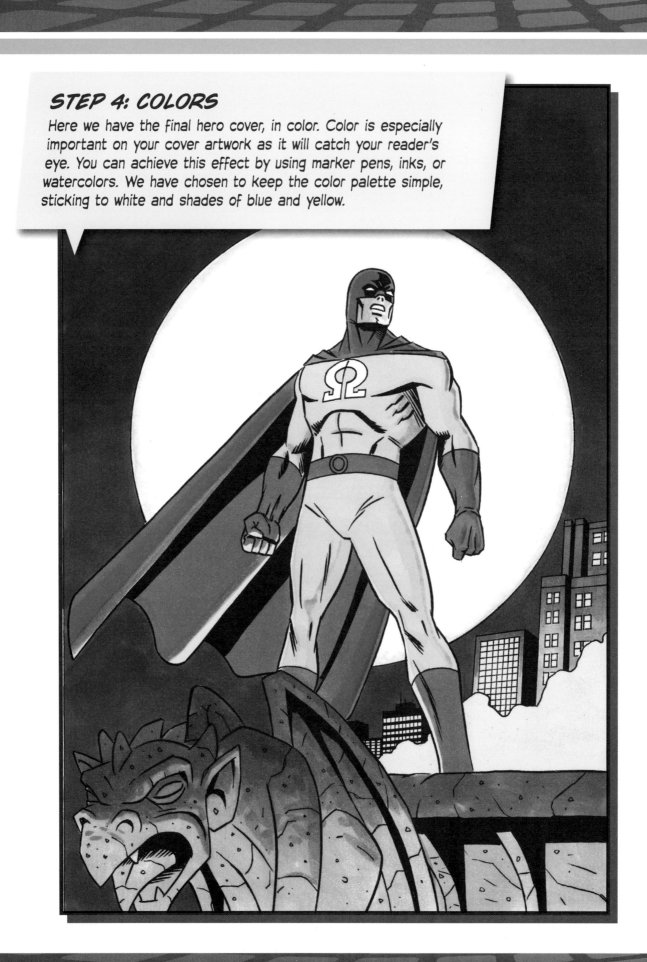

STEP 4: COLORS

Here we have the final hero cover, in color. Color is especially important on your cover artwork as it will catch your reader's eye. You can achieve this effect by using marker pens, inks, or watercolors. We have chosen to keep the color palette simple, sticking to white and shades of blue and yellow.

LIGHT SOURCES

The first thing to keep in mind as you start to apply color is the light source. In this image there are several: the moon, the street lights, and the office-building windows.

HEROIC HUES

The main body of the hero's costume is a very pale blue. Royal blue has been used for the cape, mask, and gloves. Slightly darker shades of blue have been applied for shading.

MOONLIGHT

The moon itself has been left in white and acts as the perfect bright frame for the main character.

STREET LIGHTS

Yellow tones have been added to establish the second light source. They are applied to create highlights on the gargoyle and to emphasize some outer areas of the hero's figure.

COVER DESIGN

THE CLIFFHANGER

THE STORY COVER ATTRACTS THE ATTENTION OF THE READER BY GIVING A GLIMPSE OF THE STORY INSIDE. USUALLY, IT'S THE MOST EXCITING PART OF THE PLOT THAT MAKES IT ON TO THIS TYPE OF COVER. THE READER SHOULD WANT TO READ THE COMIC BOOK TO FIND OUT WHAT HAPPENS NEXT.

STEP 1: ROUGHS

In these two thumbnail roughs, our hero is in deep trouble. The question is: which image do you think will make readers most excited?

FIRST ROUGH

Here a supervillain has our hero on the ropes. Can Omegaman possibly defeat such a powerful foe? Showing the hero in pitched battle always makes for an exciting comic-book cover.

SECOND ROUGH

In this alternate cover, the stakes have been raised. Now the supervillain has seemingly defeated the hero. The hero has been deliberately made to look small and lifeless in comparison to the maniacal monster. Will Omegaman survive to fight another day? This type of dramatic cover makes the reader eager to buy the comic book to find out the hero's fate.

STEP 2: PENCILS

We've decided to use the second rough as the basis for our final cover since it feels more shocking. The focal point is the villain, who is almost filling the page, forcing the hero toward the edge. Notice that we have changed the direction in which the hero is facing, so he looks down and away from the villain, making him appear truly defeated.

STEP 3: INKS

When inking the two characters, use a variety of different line thicknesses to prevent the drawing from looking flat. Keep your ink work clean and avoid overworking the drawing by adding unnecessary detail. The buildings don't play a significant part in this composition, so they can be inked solidly in black, with the windows left white. As with the hero cover, the sky has been left blank so there is room to add color.

STEP 4: COLORS

This image has been colored using markers, layering darker colors over pale ones. The mainly purple color palette is simple but dramatic.

INDIGO SKY

First, a bold purple is applied to the sky to set the nighttime scene. Leaving the moon as a white disc creates a spotlight effect and leaves you free to use strong colors for the hero and villain.

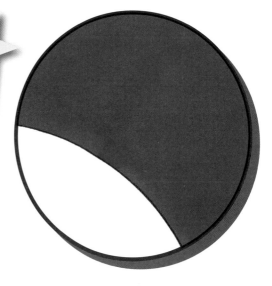

HIGHLIGHTS

Highlights are added to the monster's suit to show how it reflects the moonlight. Yellow tones are used to create the glow of street lights on the wall of the building beneath the characters.

CRIMINAL COLORS

The monster is colored by applying light blue followed by layers of lavender gray. These colors create the base color of its suit. Cadmium yellow is used for the metallic parts of the suit. Cool gray is used for the monster's boots.

COVER DESIGN

THE TEASER

THE TEASER COVER IS USED IN A SIMILAR WAY TO THE STORY COVER, TO GIVE THE READER A TASTE OF WHAT TO EXPECT WITHIN THE COMIC BOOK. THE DIFFERENCE IS THAT THE TEASER INTENTIONALLY LEAVES OUT SOME INFORMATION SO THE READER IS LEFT GUESSING.

STEP 1: ROUGHS
Once again, we tried two different approaches before settling on a favorite.

FIRST ROUGH
A muscular arm holds aloft an emblem torn from the hero's costume. It is left to the reader to wonder what has happened. Does this mean that Omegaman has been defeated? Has he even survived the confrontation?

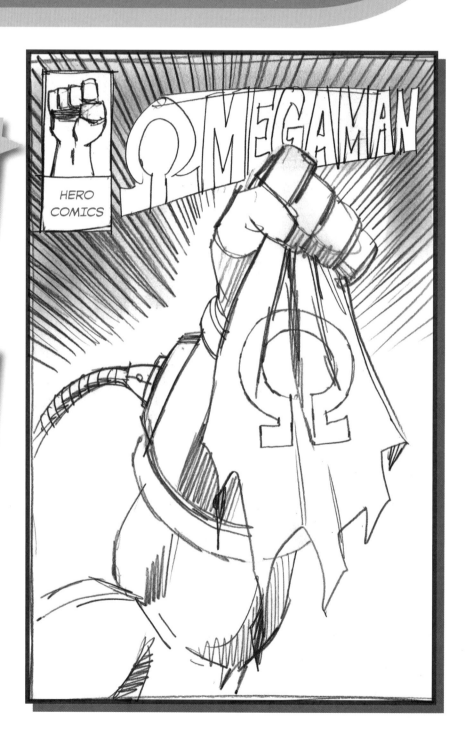

SECOND ROUGH

Here the villain is deliberately shown from an unusual angle and cast in shadow. This creates a sense of mystery. Readers might be able to figure out the identity of the villain by looking closely at the details on his outfit, but they'll have to work a little harder than if they were looking at a hero or a story cover.

STEP 2: PENCILS

This final cover may be simple in terms of the amount of detail shown, but the perspective makes it look very different to the usual fight scene. The low angle and heavy use of shading make it appear that the villain is an enormous dark presence looming over the hero.

STEP 3: INKS

You'll need plenty of ink for this cover composition! The villain is shaded almost completely in solid black and the hero is partly obscured by the position of the villain's leg. In this example, the inking stage is almost the most important one as there's very little space left for color. Despite its simplicity, this cover design will be powerful and dramatic.

STEP 4: COLORING

As this is a simple composition with a lot of heavily inked areas, the color palette must be carefully chosen to produce the most exciting effect.

RED LIGHT SPELLS DANGER

We have chosen to use a bright, attention-grabbing red background for our teaser cover, which will contrast dramatically with the black ink. Also, as we're not showing any detail in the background, we can choose a color that's symbolic of the action. Red is often used to alert the reader to potential danger. It's the perfect backdrop for the battle between our hero and villain.

Here are some questions to ask yourself as you design a cover.

- Will your cover design grab the reader's attention?

- Have you left enough space in which to add the type?

- Do your colors work together and do they reflect the message you want to communicate?

COVER DESIGN

A SCI-FI COVER

THE COVER OF A COMIC OR GRAPHIC NOVEL IS ITS MOST IMPORTANT ILLUSTRATION. IT'S THE ADVERT FOR YOUR ADVENTURE! IF YOU BREAK THE COVER DOWN INTO ITS INDIVIDUAL PARTS, YOU'LL SOON REALISE THAT IT'S LESS DIFFICULT THAN IT SEEMS AT FIRST.

STEP 1

Start with the wireframe of your central character—we have chosen space pirate Xara. Then fill the rest of the cover with supporting characters. You can use other elements to create drama, as we have done with the spaceship and the giant enemy looming in the background.

STEP 2

Now flesh out your characters. Start with the foreground and work back, so that you know how much of any element is hidden by what's in front. Add some rough background detail, such as the building outlines and the billowing smoke cloud.

STEP 3

Add more detail to your characters. The mighty mecha, Giganaut, has less detail since he is farther away. Dream up a face for your huge villain. Give the scene some action with a couple of missiles shooting past.

STEP 4

When you add ink, be careful not to go overboard. A large scene like this needs less detail on the background items, so that they don't draw attention away from, or clash with, your main characters.

STEP 5

The whole scene is brightly lit from behind by the explosions. Vary the color of large areas, such as the sky. We have left a space at the top for the title of the comic. What will you call your masterpiece?

COVER DESIGN

HORROR AND MANGA

THE FOUR COVERS THAT WE HAVE CREATED SO FAR HAVE ALL DRAWN ON SUPERHERO CONVENTIONS, AND ALL HAVE USED THE SAME STEP-BY-STEP PROCESS. OVER THE NEXT FEW PAGES WE WILL SHOWCASE SOME OTHER APPROACHES TO COVER DESIGN.

STEP 1: ROUGH COMPOSITION

Having already figured out the look of the central character, this artist has experimented with different simple shapes for the cover composition. The image on the left has a single large spiral shape curling in toward the monster. The image on the right is broken up by jagged and pointed shapes. Which do you think works best?

STEP 2: ROUGH COLORS

For this second stage, the artist has roughed up a small thumbnail of the color image to make sure that the colors he has chosen work well together. He could make several of these to see which works best.

STEP 3: FINISHED COVER

Now that the artist has decided on the composition and colors, he goes through the usual steps of penciling, inking, and coloring the cover.

CREATING A SENSE OF SPEED AND MOVEMENT

This artist wants to create the impression that a martial artist manga character is leaping out of the page right toward the reader. The cover type will appear at the bottom.

NORMAL PERSPECTIVE

UPWARD PERSPECTIVE

(The red dot shows the vanishing point, where the lines of perspective meet.)

DOWNWARD PERSPECTIVE

STEP 1: ROUGH COMPOSITION

The artist has mapped out lines of perspective with a ruler and placed a high-kicking character in various different positions over them. After careful consideration, he decides that the bottom left image has the best sense of movement and drama.

STEP 2: ROUGH COLORS

One way of making it seem as though a still image is moving is to use a technique called speed lines. These lines give us the sense that the background is blurring as we watch an object in the foreground moving at great speed. The speed lines here follow the same lines of perspective as the rest of the objects in the room. The martial artist's vivid red suit has been chosen to make her stand out against the calm background colors.

STEP 3: FINISHED COVER

Here is the final inked and colored cover image. As a finishing touch, the artist has used yet another technique for showing speed. This is called after images. These images follow behind the character like echoes. The idea is that they make it seem as though the character is moving so fast that you can barely keep track of where they are.

GLOSSARY

chiaroscuro A bold contrast between light and dark.

chibis Childlike caricatures used in manga to express characters' emotions.

color palette A selection of colors that have been chosen for a picture.

composition How the elements of an artwork or a comic-book page are arranged to make them look appealing.

foreshortening A visual effect that makes an object appear shorter than it is due to the angle it is viewed at.

layering Placing objects or colors over each other.

light source Where the light in a picture is coming from, such as a street lamp. The source itself might not be included in the picture.

manga A style of comic book and animation that first appeared in Japan.

martial artist An expert in a skilful fighting sport such as kung fu.

perspective A way of drawing items so that they look correctly sized and shaped in relation to each other and in relation to the point from which they are being viewed.

speed lines Lines that indicate movement of a character.

splash page Full-page opening panel that often begins a comic-book story.

thumbnail A small, rough sketch.

tone A shade of a color, such as light blue or dark green.

type Text that appears in books, comics, or newspapers. The type on the cover of a graphic novel usually includes the title and the name of the author.

wireframe Rough guidelines showing the pose and proportions of a figure.

vanishing point The point at which perspective lines come together.

FURTHER READING

The Art of Drawing Manga by Ben Krefta (Arcturus Publishing, 2009)

The Drawing Lesson by Mark Crilley (Random House USA, 2016)

How to Draw Comic Book Heroes by Mark Bergin (Book House, 2010)

Stan Lee's How to Draw Comics by Stan Lee (Watson–Guptill, 2010)

The Ultimate Guide to Creating Comics by William Potter and Juan Calle (Arcturus, 2017)

Write Your Own Graphic Novel by Natalie M Rosinsky (Capstone Press, 2009)

You Can Do a Graphic Novel by Barbara Slate (Alpha Books, 2010)

WEBSITES

Drawing Comics and Anime
www.drawcomics.net

Drawing Comics: Video Tutorials
www.ehow.com/video_4754254_draw-comics.html

Drawing Manga: Video Tutorials
www.youtube.com/user/markcrilley

Making Comics
www.makingcomics.com

INDEX